Oil to Cash

Oil to Cash

Fighting the Resource Curse through Cash Transfers

TODD MOSS

CAROLINE LAMBERT

STEPHANIE MAJEROWICZ

CENTER FOR GLOBAL DEVELOPMENT
Washington, D.C.

Oil to Cash: Fighting the Resource Curse through Cash Transfers may be ordered from:
BROOKINGS INSTITUTION PRESS, c/o HFS, P.O. Box 50370,
Baltimore, MD 21211-4370
Tel.: 800/537-5487; 410/516-6956
Fax: 410/516-6998 Internet: www.brookings.edu

Library of Congress Cataloging-in-Publication data

Moss, Todd J., 1970-
    Oil to cash : fighting the resource curse through cash transfers / Todd
Moss, Caroline Lambert, and Stephanie Majerowicz.
        pages   cm
    Includes bibliographical references.
    ISBN 978-1-933286-69-3
1. Natural resources. 2. Transfer payments. 3. Petroleum industry and
trade. 4. Poverty. 5. Economic development. I. Title.
    HC85.M697 2015
    339.5'22—dc23   2015002190

9 8 7 6 5 4 3 2 1

Typeset in Sabon and Strayhorn

Composition by R. Lynn Rivenbark
Macon, Georgia

Contents

Preface

The discovery of oil, minerals, or some other windfall in a developing country is potentially hugely beneficial. But it is also, simultaneously, potentially calamitous. While countries could put any new bonus revenues toward building much-needed schools and roads, fixing and staffing health systems, and policing the streets, many resource-rich states fare little better—and often much worse—than their resource-poor counterparts. Too often, newly arriving public money is misused, and funds meant to be saved are instead raided. Citizens living in poor resource-rich countries pay the price. Too often, the political system, rather than working to provide services and collect taxes, becomes obsessed with merely capturing and handing out rents. While this so-called resource curse is well known, solutions to counteract its corrosive effects have remained highly elusive.

Responding to windfall income is not just a developing-country problem; increasingly it is an issue for the international community, which has to adjust to these challenges via tax rules, transparency initiatives, aid programs, and the myriad ways it supports—and often hinders—the growth and development of fragile states. The rise of extractive income sources during boom times, and the decline during commodity price downturns, affects global relations and the prospects for the world's poor. For these reasons, both in countries reaping windfalls and for the larger global system, the Center for Global Development has taken a keen interest in the effects new resource revenue has on developing countries.

CGD's Oil-to-Cash initiative has been exploring one policy option that may help to address the root mechanism of the resource curse: handing the money directly to citizens as a way to protect the social contract between the government and its people. Under this proposal, a government would transfer some or all of the revenue from natural resource extraction to citizens in universal, transparent, and regular dividends based on clear rules. The state would treat these payments as income and tax it accordingly, forcing the state to collect taxes and creating pressure for public accountability and more responsible resource management. Since about 2009, CGD has written or commissioned work on the Oil-to-Cash concept, the political and economic dimensions, implementation considerations, and country cases spanning Asia, Latin America, the Middle East, and Africa.

This book by Todd Moss, Caroline Lambert, and Stephanie Majerowicz brings it all together. They explain the idea of Oil-to-Cash and its potential benefits, summarize the evidence on cash transfers, explain the literature on the resource curse, respond to the most common objections, and propose some initial thoughts on where Oil-to-Cash might be most appropriate. The book makes a serious contribution to the literature by clarifying for the first time in such a comprehensive manner the potential complementarity of cash transfers in poor countries with the challenges of the resource curse.

The authors' purpose is not to lay out a blueprint for countries to follow, or a shovel-ready program to implement. Instead, they aim to put a sweeping new approach on the table for public debate and for consideration by policymakers. Ultimately, they hope to enrich the way citizens, policymakers, and politicians think about the challenges and their array of options when a country suddenly receives unexpected income. Given the sad history of so many squandered resource gains in the past and the growing number of countries facing this policy dilemma, a radical idea may be just what's needed.

NANCY BIRDSALL
President
Center for Global Development

Acknowledgments

We'd like to thank the many people who contributed, however unwittingly, to the ideas in this book, especially authors of previous papers in the Oil-to-Cash series, including Caroline Decker, Shanta Devarajan, Adam Dixon, Hélène Ehrhart, Alan Gelb, Alexandra Gillies, Antony Goldman, Tuan Minh Le, Francisco Monaldi, Ashby Monk, José Morales, Arvind Nair, Gaël Raballand, Pedro Rodríguez, Aaron Sayne, Johnny West, and Lauren Young. Special appreciation goes to those who provided comments on earlier drafts of the book manuscript, especially Michael Ross, Roberto Laserna, Alan Gelb, Nancy Birdsall, Shanta Devarajan, Francisco Monaldi, Antoine Heuty, and Ryan Edwards. We also appreciate the intellectual contributions of Arvind Subramanian and Larry Diamond.

We'd like to thank John Osterman for shepherding the manuscript into its final form and Emily Schabacker for her editing magic. Todd Moss especially thanks Larry Smith for introducing him to Governor Jay Hammond's family, and Clem Tillian, Dave McRae, Bella Hammond, Pam Brodie, and Scott Goldsmith for sharing their insights into Alaska's experiences with the Permanent Fund Dividend that gave rise to the companion book, *The Governor's Solution: How Alaska's Oil Dividend Could Work in Iraq and Other Oil-Rich Countries* (Center for Global Development, 2012).

We are grateful to supporters of this project at the Center for Global Development, especially the UK Department for International Development, the Norwegian Ministry of Foreign Affairs, the Australian government, and the William and Flora Hewlett Foundation.

1

Pity the Lottery Winner

Imagine for a moment that you are a citizen of a developing country. Your country may have had a rocky time since independence, but democracy is starting to take root, and you are increasingly confident about the future. Your fellow citizens are still mostly poor, but better farming techniques and a growing manufacturing base are helping to boost wages. Your government gets its income not directly from individuals but from taxes on traded goods and a few corporations, plus a regular top-up from foreign donors. Today, however, you've received some startling news: an oil company has made a major discovery in your territorial waters. It is so significant, you are told, that within a few years oil will be your country's principal export and the single largest source of government revenue. In short, you've just won the oil lottery.

At first, this is welcome news. The oil windfall will likely bring a billion dollars or more into your government's coffers. You imagine how this new cash bonanza will drive investment to spur the rest of the economy too, paying for much-needed infrastructure, creating jobs, and raising incomes. Perhaps oil-fueled prosperity could be around the corner?

But after the initial euphoria, reality sets in. You look around at your neighbors and see that natural resource windfalls have not worked out so well for them. The risks of winning the lottery come into focus. Will oil squeeze out farming and manufacturing? Will your government be able to handle the new money? Your nation's schools and hospitals are desperate for more resources, but will any of the benefits actually reach the people? Or will the sudden cash infusion ignite a feeding frenzy of corruption among the politicians? Could fighting over oil revenues stoke political tensions, or even spark conflict?

How can you ensure that the windfall is used properly? What will your government do? What are your options?

This hypothetical dilemma has today become a reality for a growing number of countries, among them Timor-Leste, Ghana, Kenya, Papua New Guinea, Tanzania, Mozambique, Liberia, and Sierra Leone, to name just a few of the oil-and-gas newcomers. It also highlights vital policy questions for countries already deep into the difficulties of managing natural resource windfalls, such as Bolivia, Nigeria, Venezuela, Chad, Libya, Mongolia, Gabon, and Equatorial Guinea.

Most politicians facing this challenge believe their leadership can withstand the pressures of a sudden windfall. Governments in resource-rich countries are usually confident that they are capable enough to negotiate and manage contracts with oil companies, properly account for the new income, and spend the newfound wealth efficiently. But the odds are stacked against them. Too many resource-rich countries have become development-poor. And the list of new oil or gas exporters includes some of the world's poorest and most fragile states, making the downside risks especially high.

Of course, lessons can be learned from countries that have successfully managed natural resource income and thrived. Australia, Norway, Canada, Chile, and Botswana have all fared well from extracting minerals and hydrocarbons. They are also keen to share their experiences with the new producers. The International Monetary Fund and the World Bank, multilateral organizations that monitor the economic progress of developing countries and dole out advice, have also been thinking hard about policy pitfalls, and stand ready to advise governments. A mounting number of impressive civil society organizations are determined to break the so-called resource curse and have bolstered both the research and popular understanding of these risks.

There is, however, an unfortunate dearth of practical solutions. The standard conclusion from cross-country comparisons is that in order to spend unearned income well and protect a country's political integrity from the pressures of a windfall, a country must build strong institutions. This is probably true. But it is also almost always useless advice. Telling a weak country to build robust institutions is like telling an insomniac to get more sleep. The advice is correct but hardly helpful.

Much more constructive and promising is a basket of policy recommendations to boost transparency. Countries are frequently advised to publish oil contracts, join the Extractive Industries Transparency Initiative by releasing detailed data on revenues, and open up about how public money is spent. Perhaps they are also encouraged to set up a stabilization fund or some offshore financial structure to promote fiscal responsibility and protect the economy from wild swings in oil prices. These are all sound suggestions and provide specific steps a government can take to try to improve its chances of success.

Yet, while promoting greater transparency is a good idea and probably necessary, is it sufficient to crack the resource curse? Transparency alone could mitigate the potential harm of an oil jackpot in some places where actors working in the public interest are strong and can use this information to push the government toward an appropriate course. But increasing the *supply* of information where there is a scarcity of *demand* for that information will do little to hold the government accountable. In many countries where civil society has only limited influence on government, the incentives to use the information to promote better governance are weak.

In large part, the lack of accountability between a government and its people in resource-rich countries stems from the absence of a social contract. The bargain that usually ties those in power to the citizenry has been severed: citizens don't pay taxes, and the government doesn't provide quality public services. As a result, people don't expect much from their government, and public officials don't care what the people think. If the bulk of a government's income arrives gift-wrapped from a foreign company, then why bother taxing the people? Why bother with the people at all?

Even worse than indifference, opaque contracting and budget systems are, in many countries, no accidental oversight. They operate that way by design. Political interests benefit from a lack of transparency. Those reaping rents from the status quo will fight to keep their preferential access. And the rent-seeking and corruption that may already exist will only be amplified with the oil lottery winnings. If sharks are already circling the country, the oil cash is like blood thrown in the water.

Might a radically different approach to handling an oil windfall bring clear, tangible benefits to the population? Could the potential negative political dynamics be turned upside down by using the new income to boost incentives for good governance? Oil-to-Cash is a three-step proposal: (1) to create a separate fund to receive windfall revenues; (2) to give all citizens a direct stake in the country's wealth by distributing a significant portion of the new income directly to the people in a regular, universal, and transparent payment based on a set of agreed-on fiscal rules; and (3) to use the dividend mechanism to build a tax base.

A long chain of events must unfold between the discovery of offshore oil deep in the sea (or minerals deep in the ground) and the achievement of welfare-enhancing development outcomes, such as healthy, educated children or a wealthier, longer-living population. Instead of citizens hoping that the government will fulfill its duties efficiently all along this chain—that oil money will eventually turn into new roads, teachers, or vaccines as they are needed—governments can give a portion of the funds directly to the people. A large amount of evidence from cash transfer programs shows that well-designed initiatives that distribute cash directly to families can have tremendous development effects. Ordinary citizens, given extra cash, have shown themselves able to use it wisely—often more wisely than politicians, even those who have the public interest in mind.

Just as important as the direct benefits for the populace, Oil-to-Cash could also improve governance by creating citizen shareholders. When people own a portion of the profits by becoming direct shareholders in their nation's wealth, they are far more likely to pay attention. If citizens know that their wallet will be affected by the contract their government signs or by other decisions made by politicians, they have greater incentive to scrutinize the government's actions and to mobilize if things go wrong. This bond is enhanced if citizens are also turned into taxpayers, that is, if the oil dividend is used to help rebuild the social contract.

That is the idea behind Oil-to-Cash, and the idea explored in this book. While we principally apply it to the dividend from oil revenues, the concept applies equally to any windfall gained by historical or geological luck: to the discovery of gas in places like Timor-Leste and Mozambique, to revenues from mining in Zambia and Mongolia, or even to financial windfalls derived from being strategically located, as we find in Djibouti and Panama.

The next chapter reviews evidence from hundreds of cash transfer programs, examining what works, what design issues are relevant, and what we don't yet know. The advent of cash transfers, combined with rigorous program evaluation, is perhaps the most exciting change in the development business in recent memory. Chapter 3 summarizes the academic debate on the so-called resource curse, exploring various accounts of the potential harm windfall revenues can inflict and some caveats concerning popular notions of the curse. While no country's destiny is preordained by an oil find, the risks are great enough that continuing just as before and hoping for the best is likely to be a more dangerous option than trying something new.

Chapters 4 and 5 are the heart of this book. Chapter 4 explains the three-step sequence of the proposal and the practical component of implementing Oil-to-Cash. Chapter 5 explores some of the possible political and economic benefits of a national oil dividend and some indirect benefits potentially associated with it. Chapter 6 lists the ten most common objections to Oil-to-Cash and provides counterarguments. Chapter 7 concludes with an analysis of where Oil-to-Cash might make the most sense. If you are a citizen or a policymaker or an oil company executive or a president, is the option worth exploring in your own country?

Our aim in writing this book is not to provide a one-size-fits-all blueprint that any country can roll out to deal with an unexpected windfall. Any program that links income from natural resources with direct cash transfers to citizens must be carefully tailored to the multiple and complex specifics of each country. The conditions on the ground, the state of current institutions, the profile of the revenue source, and especially the preferences of the population all need to be taken into account.

While the idea of oil dividends may at first appear radical, Oil-to-Cash is in essence an attempt to restore some kind of normalcy in state-citizen relations in countries where the balance of power between citizens and their government has been upended by the sudden inflow of oil revenue. In fact, all the elements of Oil-to-Cash are already being implemented somewhere. Our hope is that by pulling them together, we can make a modest contribution to the challenge of dealing with sudden oil wealth. Our aim is to bring together some of the latest thinking on public policy to try to tackle in a hardheaded way one of the great policy dilemmas facing political leaders today. If the resource lottery is mishandled, if the tools provided are inadequate to the task, then the tremendous progress made over the past half century is put at risk, and the world will collectively miss an opportunity to bolster governance and development outcomes in some of the world's most troubled places. At a minimum, we hope to provide food for thought and some new options for our hypothetical citizen facing perhaps one of the toughest public policy conundrums.

2

Giving Money Directly to the Poor

"If a free society cannot help the many who are poor, it cannot save the few who are rich."

—John F. Kennedy

Oil-to-Cash rests in part on the idea that distributing oil revenues directly to citizens will advance development more effectively and more equitably than funneling revenues straight into government coffers. But is this assumption true? After all, governments have years of experience managing budgets for health, education, and other services. Does transferring cash directly to citizens really provide any greater benefit?

The evidence in support of cash transfers is ample and growing. Countries in Africa, Latin America, and Asia have been experimenting with cash transfers for years. In many cases the direct transfer of cash to citizens, when properly conceived and executed, has been highly effective in improving the lives of the poor. This chapter gathers evidence from such initiatives around the world and considers what we know and don't know about designing and implementing effective cash transfer programs.

The Poverty Trap

In the war on poverty, battles are being won. In the early 1980s, more than half the population of the developing world, or a staggering 1.9 billion people, lived in poverty.[1] That figure fell sharply in the decade leading

---

1. Poverty is defined here as living on less than $1.25 a day in 1995 prices. See World Bank (2014).

up to 2005, and by 2010 the proportion was one in five. Extreme poverty is projected to retreat even further by 2015.

Yet even if the current rate of progress is maintained, some 1 billion people will still be living in extreme poverty in 2015.[2] In addition, progress has been uneven. Most of the stunning success has occurred in East Asia, where the poverty rate has plummeted. The picture is not as rosy in India and large parts of sub-Saharan Africa, where poverty rates are still stubbornly high. Chronic poverty, defined as extreme and long-term poverty that often spans several generations, also remains unacceptably high. Between 320 million and 443 million people alive today will spend most or all of their lives destitute, with little hope of an improvement in their situation.[3]

For those fortunate enough to escape extreme poverty, the risk of backsliding is ever present. Illness, accident, and the deaths of family earners or caregivers routinely set back those who have barely climbed out of poverty. Economic downturns and fluctuations in international prices make matters worse. The global financial and economic crises pushed an estimated 50 million more people into poverty in 2009, and a further 64 million people in 2010.[4] Climate change is also making it harder to escape poverty. Millions of people who depend on rain-fed agriculture or who live in flood-prone areas are becoming ever more vulnerable. The number of poor people affected by climate disasters is predicted to rise steeply.[5]

Spurred by recent economic shocks, governments and donors are looking to build more responsive social protection programs. Increasingly, they are turning to a promising new tool: cash transfers. Since 2000, a growing number of developing countries have introduced cash transfer programs. More recently, donors and multilateral development banks have begun championing these programs. Cash transfer programs have spread from a few middle-income countries to all regions of the world. Today, between 750 million and 1 billion people[6] in at least forty-five developing countries[7] receive money directly from their governments.

2. World Bank (2014).
3. Chronic Poverty Research Centre (2008).
4. World Bank (2010).
5. DFID-UK (2011).
6. DFID-UK (2011).
7. Hanlon, Barrientos, and Hulme (2010).

TABLE 2-1. Selected Cash Transfer Programs in Low- and Middle-Income Countries

Country	Program	No. of recipients
Argentina	Jefes y Jefas de Hogar	1,500,000
Bolivia	Bonosol/Renta Dignidad	800,000
Botswana	Old-age pension	80,000
China	Minimum Livelihood Guarantee (di Bao)	22,000,000
Colombia	Cajas de Compensación Familiar	3,900,000
	Prospera pension	380,961
Kenya	Hunger Safety Net	60,000
Lesotho	Old Age Pension Program	69,046
Malawi	Dowa Emergency Cash Transfer	10,161
Mauritius	Old Age Pension	109,000
Mozambique	INAS Food Subsidy	69,095
Pakistan	Benazir Income Support	2,200,000
South Africa	Child Support Grant	8,893,999
	Older Person's Grant	2,309,679
	Disability Grant	1,377,466
Swaziland	Save the Children Swaziland emergency cash transfer	6,223

Why Cash Transfers?

The design, scale, and objectives of cash transfer programs vary. Some programs provide cash without conditions, while others impose conditions such as school attendance or health clinic visits. Some cash transfer programs target particular demographic groups, such as children, orphans, the elderly, or the disabled, while others focus on people able to work. Latin America, which pioneered cash transfer programs, has typically focused on improving child health and education and on discouraging child labor. In sub-Saharan Africa, programs tend to be geared toward alleviating food insecurity, HIV/AIDS-related problems, and chronic poverty. In almost all cases, cash transfer programs seek to address one or more of the causes of poverty, whether it is a lack of cash, an unpredictable income, limited access to schools, poor health, or inadequate nutrition (see table 2-1).

By now, many cash transfer programs have been examined, dissected, and evaluated. Most of the scrutiny has fallen on programs in the relatively wealthier developing countries, where transfers have been in place for some time and where money and research capacity are available.

But smaller and newer programs in poorer countries have also come under the microscope. In a great variety of locations, the emerging picture is extremely promising: under the right circumstances, giving money directly to people is one of the most effective ways to help them escape poverty. The most prominent reasons for direct cash transfers are detailed below.

Cash Transfers Reduce Chronic Poverty and Inequality

Being poor means trying to survive on an income that is both small and unpredictable. When people do not know how much money they will have tomorrow, next week, or next month, it becomes impossible to plan. Families struggle to keep their children in school, and hesitate to seek treatment when they are ill. They cannot borrow and they cannot invest. And when disaster strikes—whether in the form of a bad harvest, or an illness, or too much or too little rain—families cope by eating less, selling possessions, and withdrawing children from school so they can work.

A predictable income, even a small one, affords the breathing space to ease, or sometimes to escape, poverty. The impact of cash transfer programs on poverty is well documented. South Africa's cash grants, for instance, have reduced the depth of poverty by almost half,[8] while Mexico's poverty gap[9] declined by about a fifth following the introduction of the Progresa cash transfer program, later renamed Oportunidades.[10] Although impacts vary according to how they are measured, there is little doubt that cash transfers directly improve the lives of the poor.

Besides easing poverty, cash transfers help narrow inequalities. Mexico's Oportunidades and Brazil's Bolsa Família, for instance, have helped to significantly reduce the gap between rich and poor. These programs were responsible for more than one-fifth of the inequality reduction observed between the mid-1990s and 2004, as measured by the Gini coefficient.[11] The impact of direct cash transfers on Brazil's income gap

8. Samson and others (2004).

9. The average shortfall between household income and the poverty line.

10. Fiszbein and Schady (2009). Created in 1997, Progresa was the first conditional cash transfer program piloted in Mexico; its careful impact evaluation spurred the popularity of similar programs around the world. In 2001 the program was scaled up, and the following year it was renamed Oportunidades (www.undp.org/content/dam/undp/library/Poverty%20Reduction/Participatory%20Local%20Development/Mexico_Progresa_web.pdf).

11. Soares and others (2009); Veras Soares and others (2006).

was even greater when a broader range of national cash transfers (beyond Bolsa Família) was considered. The programs were found to be responsible for one-third of the decline in inequality between 2001 and 2007[12] and for 28 percent of the reduction in the Gini coefficient between 1995 and 2004.[13] Similarly, South Africa's cash grants reduced inequality by three percentage points and doubled the share of national income captured by the poorest 20 percent of the population.[14]

Cash Transfers Improve Nutrition

Cash transfer recipients tend to eat more and eat better than poor people who do not receive transfers. When poor people receive money, they spend it primarily on food, especially in low-income countries. On average, about half of the value of cash transfers is spent on food.[15] But in Malawi and Ethiopia, recipients spend more than three-fourths of their cash transfers on groceries.[16] In Lesotho, almost half of pensioners report never going hungry, compared to 19 percent before the Old Age Pension Program—a cash transfer program designed to help the elderly—was introduced. Families that receive social grants in South Africa are less hungry than families with a comparable income that do not receive grants.[17]

Besides eating more, those who receive cash transfers also consume greater quantities of protein and produce. Households participating in Malawi's Mchinji program ate meat or fish two days a week, while nonparticipating households ate meat or fish only once every three weeks. In Zambia, cash transfer recipients were found to eat more protein.[18] Families enrolled in Colombia's Familias en Acción began eating more meat, milk, and eggs, while in Mexico and Nicaragua, recipients spend more on meat, fruits, and vegetables than do nonrecipients.[19]

12. Hailu and Soares (2009). Various cash transfers were taken into account, including the lowest level of contributory pension system, partially contributory rural pensions, noncontributory income substitution for those unable to work and who live in poor families, and Bolsa Família.
13. Veras Soares and others (2006). The study measured the impact of both Bolsa Família and Benefício de Prestação Continuada, the means-tested old-age pension and disability grant.
14. Samson, van Niekerk, and Mac Quene (2011).
15. DFID-UK (2011).
16. Yablonski and O'Donnell (2009).
17. Samson and others (2004).
18. Vincent and Cull (2009).
19. Fiszbein and Schady (2009).

BOX 2-1.   Food Spending: Consumption or Investment?

Typically, economists consider expenditure on food to be consumption since it is used immediately. Consumption is technically regarded as less productive than investment, which is intended to yield future benefits. This suggests that spending more on food is less desirable than investing. For families at the very low end of the poverty spectrum, however, improved nutrition underpins better health and often improved school performance, which in turn improves labor market participation. In this context, extra consumption might therefore be better thought of as an investment in human capital.

While everyone benefits from eating greater quantities of nutritious food, children benefit the most. In South Africa, children in families receiving the Child Support Grant during their first two years of life are taller than children in families that did not receive this support during those critical first years, thanks to better nutrition.[20] In Brazil's Northeast Region, Bolsa Família has reduced chronic child malnutrition by almost half.[21] Improved nutrition supports better physical and mental development, which in turn can result in better school performance (see box 2-1).

Cash Transfers Increase School Attendance and Health Clinic Visits

Children from families receiving cash transfers also attend more school than their counterparts in families that do not receive transfers. Cash transfers have resulted in higher school enrollment both in middle-income countries such as Chile and Mexico and in low-income countries such as Honduras, Nicaragua, Bangladesh, Cambodia, and Pakistan.[22] In Cambodia, a scholarship program ensured that the 30 percent of girls who otherwise would have dropped out after primary school instead advanced to the next grade.[23]

The impact of cash transfers on school attendance is particularly pronounced for children who were attending school infrequently when the program started. Turkey's program did not affect enrollment in primary school and among boys in high school, as numbers were already high. But it significantly raised teenage girls' attendance, which was initially

20. Agüero, Carter, and Woolard (2007).
21. Cited in Hanlon, Barrientos, and Hulme (2010).
22. Fiszbein and Schady (2009).
23. Filmer and Schady (2006).

very low. Similarly, Nicaragua's intervention produced more bang for its buck than Mexico's or Colombia's, where primary school enrollment was higher before transfers started.[24]

The impact of cash transfers sometimes extends beyond the direct beneficiaries. In Mexico, children of families that were poor but not eligible for Oportunidades became more likely to stay in school because those benefiting from the program were enrolled.[25] By encouraging schooling, several cash transfer programs in Latin America and Cambodia have been associated with reductions in child labor.[26]

Although many programs are conditional on school attendance and would therefore be expected to affect the amount of schooling, cash transfers that come with no strings attached also appear to have a positive impact. South Africa's unconditional Child Support Grant, for instance, improves school attendance, particularly for children who live with their mothers.[27] Pensioners in Lesotho spend some of their pension on school fees, schoolbooks, and school transport, as well as on children's health care, food, and clothes. Children in households that receive pensions attend school more regularly and are better fed.[28]

Many cash transfer programs also require that children receive regular checkups at a health clinic. This mandate typically results in an increase in the use of health services. Programs in Colombia, Honduras, and Nicaragua with such a requirement have led to closer monitoring of the growth and development of young children. In Colombian families receiving grants from Familias en Acción, for example, more than a third more children between two and four years old were seen by a health care provider than in families not receiving such aid.[29] In Chile, Ecuador, and Mexico, by contrast, the impact appears to have been minimal. Similarly, the impact of cash transfer programs on children's immunization rates has been significant in Honduras, Nicaragua, and Turkey but much more muted in Colombia and Mexico, in part because immunizations levels were already high.[30]

---

24. Filmer and Schady (2006).
25. Filmer and Schady (2006).
26. ILO (2010) and DFID-UK (2011).
27. Williams (2007).
28. Croome, Nyanguru, and Molisana (2007).
29. Attanasio, Pellerano, and Polania (2005).
30. Fiszbein and Schady (2009).

For adults receiving cash transfers intended to improve health, the results are mixed. Some programs have little or no perceptible impact on adult use of preventive health services. But in Lesotho, more than half of old-age pension recipients reported spending more money on health care,[31] and results for families spanning multiple age groups are generally positive. Conditional cash transfer programs in eight countries have been found to improve the uptake of maternal and newborn health services such as prenatal monitoring and skilled attendance at births.[32] In Tanzania, a pilot cash transfer program successfully reduced sexually transmitted infections.[33] Similarly, eighteen months after the introduction of a cash transfer pilot program in a district in Malawi with a high HIV prevalence, the rate of infection among teenage girls enrolled in the program was 60 percent lower than among those who did not receive payments.[34]

Attending school and visiting the clinic are steps on the path out of poverty, though, as discussed later in the chapter, these steps alone do not guarantee learning or better health.

The Multiplier Effect of Cash Transfers

Although cash transfers are primarily designed to help recipients escape poverty, there is limited but compelling evidence that they also help jump-start a virtuous economic cycle. First, transfers help sustain local markets in poor and remote areas by boosting consumption. Recipients who are able to buy more food, household goods, seeds, fertilizer, or cattle often do so locally. Cash transfers in Zambia, Namibia, and Lesotho, for example, have stimulated local businesses,[35] and similar results have been observed in Brazil and in Malawi's Mchinji District.[36]

A guaranteed income covering basic needs also provides a safety net that allows poor families to take more risks. Families can invest in improved farming technology or new businesses instead of stashing money away to use in emergencies. Families in Ethiopia, Zambia,

---

31. Croome, Nyanguru, and Molisana (2007).
32. Glassman, Duran, and Koblimsky (2013).
33. De Walque and others (2010).
34. Baird (2012).
35. Samson, van Niekerk, and Mac Quene (2011).
36. Hanlon, Barrientos, and Hulme (2010).

Paraguay, and Mexico, for instance, invested part of their cash transfers in farming, livestock, and microbusinesses.[37] Recipients in Ethiopia and India buy more fertilizer and higher-yielding seeds.[38] In northern Uganda, youth who received cash to invest in training and tools earned 41 percent more within four years than those who did not, and were 65 percent more likely to engage in a skilled trade, such as carpentry, metalworking, tailoring, or hairstyling. They were also 40 percent more likely to keep records, register their business, and pay taxes.[39]

For most recipients, investing pays off, amplifying the impact of the cash transfers. Oportunidades recipients in rural Mexico who invested 12 percent of their cash transfer in agriculture or microbusinesses generated average returns of 18 percent. Five and a half years later, those families had boosted their consumption by a third, thanks to the extra income from their investments.[40] Poor rural pensioners in Bolivia, who typically have land but no cash to invest in seeds or livestock, increased their food consumption when they invested their cash transfers in producing more meat and vegetables.[41] In Zambia and Malawi, investments in farming generated jobs when recipients hired labor to plow their fields.[42]

In addition to providing cash to invest, regular transfers can open the door to credit. With few or no possessions to offer as collateral and an often unpredictable income, the poor either face prohibitive borrowing costs or are unable to borrow at all. In Brazil and Bangladesh, cash transfer programs have facilitated access to credit.[43] Reliable cash payments also help bring families into the formal banking system: in South Africa, 42 percent of people receiving Child Support Grants have a bank account, a significantly higher proportion than the 24 percent of nonrecipients at similar income levels.[44]

Although cash transfers have delivered measurable benefits to recipients, it is still hard to gauge their overall influence on a country's economy.

37. DFID-UK (2011).
38. Hanlon, Barrientos, and Hulme (2010).
39. Blattman, Fiala, and Martinez (2013).
40. Gertler, Martinez, and Rubio-Codina (2006).
41. Barrientos and Scott (2008).
42. Wietler (2007).
43. Barrientos and Scott (2008).
44. Hanlon, Barrientos, and Hulme (2010).

There is little evidence so far linking cash transfers and GDP growth one way or the other.[45]

Cash Transfers Ease Disaster Recovery

Most cash transfer programs are meant to be long-term interventions to ameliorate chronic conditions. But as these programs expand from middle-income countries to poorer parts of the globe, they are being used to respond to emergencies, replacing in-kind assistance such as food aid and shelter. Disaster-stricken families who receive cash can then decide for themselves what they need most, and these programs can smooth the transition from relief to recovery.

Ethiopia established its Productive Safety Nets Program in 2005 as a response to chronic food crises. The program provides public works jobs between January and June, when farmwork is scarce; families without a breadwinner to take advantage of these jobs receive cash. The program also offers credit and agriculture extension, and by 2008 it covered more than 7 million people. At a cost of nearly 2 percent of the national economy, it is the largest cash transfer program in the region after South Africa's.[46]

In Pakistan the safety net system was overwhelmed following floods that devastated much of the country in July and August 2010. With more than 20 million people affected, 1.6 million homes destroyed, and 2.4 million hectares of crops damaged, the government had to act fast. In September, federal and provincial authorities launched a cash grant program to assist people affected by the floods. Within three months, 1.4 million families were registered and had received an initial grant of PKR 20,000 ($230), with another 400,000 households expected to be part of the first phase. Families spent their money mainly on food, medical bills, repairs, and debt payoff. The worst-affected and most vulnerable families were expected to receive an additional PKR 40,000 in a second phase to cover basic needs, and to repair houses, recapitalize assets, and recover their destroyed livelihood.[47]

Donors are encouraging this shift to cash transfers in the wake of disasters. International financial institutions, including the World Bank, are supporting Ethiopia's and Pakistan's programs. In response to the earth-

45. DFID-UK (2011).
46. Hanlon, Barrientos, and Hulme (2010).
47. World Bank (2011).

quake in Haiti in January 2010, some relief agencies are relying on cash transfers to assist victims, and the European Union is increasingly delivering humanitarian assistance through cash and voucher programs.[48]

While cash transfers used for disaster response are fundamentally different in both scope and duration from programs seeking long-term effects, they have also demonstrated the feasibility of such programs under the most challenging circumstances.

Cash Transfers Improve the Social Contract

The poor often have little political voice. Disempowerment, poverty, and acute inequality feed tensions that weaken the state in many developing countries. Establishing a direct financial channel between the state and its poorest citizens can strengthen a country's social fabric and help build national identity.

Creating and maintaining a "social contract" is essential to political stability. Through the social contract, the state and its citizens are bound by mutual obligations: authorities are expected to provide law and order, infrastructure, and public services, in exchange for which citizens owe allegiance to the state and are expected to respect institutions and pay taxes. A breakdown of this give-and-take threatens political and social stability.

Social protection can be part of this compact. In some cases, cash transfer programs were introduced to improve national cohesion. Mexico launched its Progresa program in part to address the roots of the 1990s Chiapas uprising, while the rapid expansion of China's Minimum Livelihood Guarantee and Argentina's Jefes y Jefas de Hogar attempted to defuse threats of unrest prompted by rising unemployment.[49] Kenya extended cash transfers and dedicated significant resources to fiscal protection even during the global economic recession to promote stability following the political violence that rocked the country in 2008.[50] Similarly, Sierra Leone's and Nepal's interventions were designed to promote social cohesion and contribute to peace processes.[51]

Social protection may also strengthen community bonds and solidarity. Colombia's Familias en Acción program improved cooperation

48. DFID-UK (2011).
49. Barrientos and Hulme (2008).
50. McCord (2009).
51. Holmes (2009).

among participants in Cartagena by requiring that they participate in social activities and thereby interact.[52] Mexico's Progresa program reinforced social relationships among women covered by the program, some of whom banded together to oppose violence and abuse.[53] Participants in Chile's program became more aware of social services in their community and began to proactively seek help from local institutions, an outcome suggesting better social inclusion.[54] Pensioners in Lesotho and Namibia reported enjoying more respect and an enhanced social status thanks to their improved financial position.[55]

Little is known about the influence of cash transfers on politics, but recipients appear more likely to vote, and to vote for the politicians and parties that introduced the cash transfer program. There is some evidence that conditional cash transfers in Mexico translated into higher electoral turnout and support for the incumbent in the 2000 presidential election, even though every candidate committed to expanding the program. But this did not appear to reflect clientelism or vote buying: the distribution of federal money straight to voters actually weakened the hold of local political barons and their selective generosity.[56] In Uruguay, beneficiaries of the PANES program, or Plan de Atención Nacional a la Emergencia Social, were significantly more likely to favor the incumbent government, which had introduced the cash transfers; the effect of the transfers on political support was particularly pronounced among the poorest recipients and swing voters.[57] In Brazil, mayors who had successfully and transparently implemented cash transfers were more likely to be reelected, but the impact of cash transfers was greater in municipalities governed by first-term mayors than in municipalities with incumbents who were ineligible for reelection, suggesting strong electoral incentives to perform.[58] Bolsa Família may also have helped shift President Lula da Silva's voting base away from the more developed regions and toward the poorest areas of the country.[59]

52. Attanasio, Pellerano, and Polania (2008).
53. ILO (2010).
54. ILO (2010).
55. ILO (2010).
56. De La O (2011).
57. Manacorda, Miguel, and Vigorito (2009).
58. De Janvry, Finan, and Sadoulet (2009).
59. Zucco (2008).

What Makes Cash Transfers Work?

There is little debate that when properly designed and implemented, cash transfers work for many objectives. Those who receive money are less vulnerable and can carve a foothold out of poverty. But cash transfers are no magic bullet. They do not work in isolation, and no single formula fits all circumstances. Their design must reflect each country's objectives, poverty profile, and fiscal and skills constraints, as well as its political and social environment. In other words, successful cash transfer schemes are tailor-made, not mass-produced. Nonetheless, some lessons have emerged from the growing body of evidence around the world. The characteristics that must be considered on a country-by-country basis to make cash transfers work are described below.

Clear Objectives

The objectives of a cash transfer program should be clear from the outset, as they influence scope and design. Are transfers meant to ease immediate poverty or instead to focus on the next generation? Is the goal to achieve immediate improvements in welfare or longer-term development? Will the program support the most vulnerable—such as children, the elderly, or the disabled—or target those who can work, as a way to create a virtuous economic cycle?

Of course, a program can have more than one objective. But fiscal constraints, politics, and the nature and extent of poverty in each country demand choices, as does a country's capacity to design and implement programs. Even wealthier countries, which may have fewer fiscal and capacity restraints than their poorer counterparts, need to clearly define their objectives in light of economic and political realities.

Conditional versus Unconditional Funding

Do recipients send their kids to school and undergo health checkups because they have to, or do they do it anyway and to the same extent when cash is transferred with no strings attached? Programs that focus on reducing poverty by improving human capital tend to be conditional; many of Latin America's cash transfer programs fall into this category. Mexico's Oportunidades program, for instance, requires that mothers bring their children to health clinics for regular checkups and vaccines, and attend meetings on health and nutrition. Mothers who fail to uphold their end of the bargain lose their grants. Cash may also be conditional on school attendance. In Brazil, skipping school or failing to go to the clinic earns grant recipients a visit from social services. Supporters of conditioning grant funding on a certain set of behaviors argue that parents do not always make choices that are in their children's best interest, either because they are misinformed or because they prioritize their own interests above their children's. To prevent inherited poverty, conditional cash transfer programs aim to give children a fair start in life, beginning with access to health services and education.

In contrast, programs with a rights-based approach to social assistance often come with no strings attached. Cash transfers in sub-Saharan Africa's wealthier countries, such as South Africa's child support benefit, are all unconditional,[60] as are old-age or disability pensions in most countries.

Whether to impose conditions on cash transfers is not always an ideological choice but is often a pragmatic one. Imposing conditions for receiving grants is not only burdensome for recipients, it is also costly for governments. Verifying compliance costs money and requires a well-functioning civil service. Imposing conditions also means that adequate schools and health services must be available: requiring children to go to school if there are no schools nearby is unfair and impractical. These real-world constraints are particularly problematic in poor countries, and so it is not surprising that the overwhelming majority of cash transfer programs in low-income or fragile states in sub-Saharan Africa are unconditional.[61]

But even if conditions can feasibly be met, are they necessary? Supporters of unconditional cash transfers argue that the main reason parents do not send their children to school or take them to the clinic is either that they cannot afford to or that these services are not available. If parents actually invest in their children when given the means to do so, and if taxpayers are willing to finance unconditional cash transfers, then attaching strings to cash transfers makes little sense. Although grants that require parents to send their children to school can clearly boost attendance, what about schemes that do not? In many cases they deliver

60. Garcia and Moore (2012).
61. Garcia and Moore (2012).

the same results: in South Africa, Namibia, and Lesotho, unconditional benefits also translate into more schooling, particularly for girls.[62] In other words, it is unclear whether higher school and clinic attendance should be credited to the conditions or to the availability of cash.

A pilot scheme in Malawi's Zomba District attempted to settle this debate by comparing school attendance among families receiving conditional and unconditional cash transfers. The pilot program confirmed that cash transfers significantly improved school attendance overall. But it also concluded that the enrollment, attendance, and school results of girls who had received conditional cash transfers were higher than those of girls who benefited from unconditional grants. However, grants conditional on girls' school attendance were less effective in delaying marriage and pregnancy than unconditional grants, possibly because the attendance requirement was too onerous or failed to make education more attractive than marriage.[63] The Zomba experience illustrates that rigid conditions can potentially backfire, withdrawing social protection from poor families that may need additional help.[64]

Apart from the question of social impact, establishing conditions is sometimes politically expedient. Securing broad political support to spend public monies on the poor may be easier when grants are not perceived as free handouts but as rewards for "good" behavior. The Brazilian media's reporting on Bolsa Família illustrates this point.[65] More surprisingly, beneficiaries themselves may prefer conditional transfers, as seen in Kenya and Zambia.[66] In Zambia, conditions allowed beneficiaries to better negotiate household expenses with their spouses.

To address logistical complications and political considerations, a number of countries have adopted "soft" conditions. In these schemes, beneficiaries formally agree to a list of conditions but are not penalized if they fail to comply. This approach has been popular in sub-Saharan Africa, where conditional programs are on the rise but the capacity to

62. Garcia and Moore (2012).

63. Baird, McIntosh, and Özler (2010). These perplexing findings are even more confusing when considered in conjunction with a preliminary version of the study (Baird, McIntosh, and Özler 2009). The preliminary study reported an opposite finding: the impact, on average, was similar for both conditional and unconditional cash recipients.

64. Samson, van Niekerk, and Mac Quene (2011).

65. Fiszbein and Schady (2009).

66. Garcia and Moore (2012).

monitor compliance or to provide the extra schools and clinics needed to meet the demand created by the conditional transfers is often limited.[67]

The Supply Side: Providing the Services to Support Cash Transfers

Cash transfers cannot work in isolation. To ease poverty in the short and long term, recipients need access to markets to spend the cash they receive, and to adequate schools and clinics. This means that authorities must respond to the demand these programs create by providing not only more services but also better ones.

Expanding services requires different approaches in different contexts. Where services are already available but hard to access, expanding may only require improving access. In Chile, for instance, an adequate network of schools and health services was already available and could accommodate the relatively small number of people targeted by Chile Solidario. No expansion was necessary, but social workers coordinated with municipalities to make sure that existing services were available to beneficiaries.[68]

In most countries, however, meeting the extra demand for services requires adjusting supply and facilitating transport. Where they are not already available, governments may need to build new classrooms and clinics. Mexico, for instance, refurbished rural primary schools and built secondary schools, while mobile health teams expanded into underserved areas. Bangladesh's share of education in social spending almost doubled to expand the schooling system, and an increase in private schools also helped fill the gap. El Salvador deployed mobile brigades and nongovernmental organizations to provide basic health and nutrition services.[69] Nicaragua provided financial incentives and training to mobile health teams contracted from the private sector to visit beneficiaries, and to teachers to cover the extra workload.[70]

Yet in many developing countries, it is the quality of public services that is inadequate, and quality is harder to fix than quantity. This might explain why cash transfer programs, while resulting in a higher demand for education and health services, have so far had a less convincing impact on education and health outcomes. Although cash transfers can

67. Garcia and Moore (2012).
68. Fiszbein and Schady (2009).
69. Fiszbein and Schady (2009).
70. Moore (2009).

be credited with lower rates of illness and mortality among recipients in Malawi, Colombia, and Mexico,[71] a study of several conditional cash transfer programs in other countries found mixed impacts on illness, child mortality, height, and anemia.[72]

Targeting

Should cash transfer programs target those who need them most, or aim more broadly? Much depends on the program objectives and on a country's administrative capacity and poverty profile. Most transfers incorporate some targeting. Many programs attempt to focus on the poorest, often choosing recipients based on where they live, what they own, or how much they earn. Old-age pensions, child support grants, and disability benefits target specific demographics. Emergency programs often focus on regions worst affected by natural disasters. Most schemes combine several targeting criteria.

Mexico's Oportunidades relies primarily on a census that assigns points to families based on age, gender, and education level, as well as on access to amenities such as water and electricity and ownership of a TV or radio. In Brazil, eligibility is based on local authorities' identifying those considered low income. South Africa's Child Support Grant is distributed based on the age of the children and, in theory, income, although the means test is no longer strictly enforced as it tended to exclude too many eligible families. Lesotho's and Nepal's pensions are based on age only. Public works programs often target areas where rates of poverty, unemployment, or malnutrition are highest.

Targeting offers a significant advantage: it reduces the cost of benefits by focusing on a smaller number of recipients. Targeted schemes in Latin America typically cost less than 1 percent of GDP.[73] When properly implemented, targeting ensures that resources are spent on people who need them most. When resources are scarce, targeting also makes available larger transfers for each family rather than spreading cash thinly among a larger group of recipients, as discussed in the next section.

Yet targeting, particularly if conducted using sophisticated methods that rely on proxy means or means tests, is not always effective. It requires resources and a bureaucracy that is sophisticated enough not

71. DFID-UK (2011).
72. Fiszbein and Schady (2009).
73. DFID-UK (2011).

only to determine who should benefit from the program but to weed out abuses, too. This may not be realistic in low-income countries. Poor administration results in granting benefits to people who should not receive transfers and excluding others who should. On a large scale, these errors undermine a program's credibility and can potentially fuel social tensions.

Targeting can also create a heavy burden on potential beneficiaries, who must prove they meet the eligibility requirements. Proving one's age when official identification documents are rare, for instance, can be challenging. This is why Nepal's social pension program accepts horoscopes as proof of age when applicants cannot provide birth certificates.

Perfect targeting is difficult to achieve, and it commonly misses more than half of eligible beneficiaries. In Bangladesh, for example, only 6 percent of the eligible poor are reported to receive the government's social pension, and South Africa's Child Support Grant reached only one in ten eligible families the first few years after it was introduced.[74]

When poverty is widespread and people move in and out of its grasp repeatedly over time, the savings generated by limiting the number of beneficiaries may not outweigh the effort and cost of targeting. A study of fifteen African countries where poverty rates were extremely high found little difference between universal provision and perfect targeting.[75] Focusing exclusively on the poorest may also undermine vital political support from the rest of the population for transfers.

While income targeting is widespread in Latin America, poorer countries tend to rely on simpler forms of targeting. Several methods can be combined. Almost eight in ten cash transfer schemes in sub-Saharan Africa target demographic categories such as children and the elderly. Schemes targeting specific regions or relying on local communities to choose beneficiaries are particularly popular among low-income countries in the region.[76] Kenya's program supporting orphans and vulnerable children, for instance, identifies recipients by combining methods. Districts are first selected based on HIV prevalence, and community members then propose recipients based on defined criteria. The community's preliminary selection is sent to Nairobi, and a final decision is made after further household visits and according to community-

74. Samson, van Niekerk, and Mac Quene (2011).
75. Kakwani, Veras Soares, and Son (2005).
76. Garcia and Moore (2012).

validated rankings. Local communities also play a central role in identifying recipients in Malawi's Social Cash Transfer Program.[77]

Size

Cash transfers are often not enough to lift families out of poverty. But transfers can significantly improve a family's lot, provided they are appropriately sized and predictable. Although small amounts of cash can make a difference, transfers that are too small are unlikely to have much impact; when conditions impose extra costs, the impact is even slighter. Transfer schemes in Honduras and Mozambique were found to have little influence on nutrition, for instance, owing in part to the low transfer value.[78] In both cases the value of the grants was less than 10 percent of the poverty line.[79]

By some estimates, grants need to increase family consumption by at least 10 percent to be perceived as useful and by 15–20 percent to make a significant difference.[80] The right level of benefits depends largely on program objectives and fiscal resources. The value of transfers meant primarily to deal with short-term poverty, for example, often reflects poverty thresholds. Lesotho's Old Age Pension was set at the equivalent of $25, or the national poverty line for one person.[81] Programs that focus on changing behavior toward schooling usually consider the cost of education, from the cost of school fees, uniforms, and transportation to the forgone revenue from child labor. Likewise, the price of food influences the value of transfers meant to improve nutrition. The benefits of Zambia's Kalomo pilot project—equivalent to $6 a month, or $8 for families with children—were meant to cover the cost of one meal a day. The Latin American standard is 20 percent of the average household consumption for the target population.

Regardless of size, payments should be indexed to inflation, or benefits will erode over time. Another consideration in determining transfer size is the presence (or absence) of family caps. Some programs have paid per child, since larger families have greater expenses and are generally poorer. However, because of possible concerns about fertility

77. Handa and others (2012).
78. DFID-UK (2011).
79. Yablonski and O'Donnell (2009).
80. Hanlon, Barrientos, and Hulme (2010).
81. Samson, van Niekerk, and Mac Quene (2011).

incentives, most Latin American programs (Honduras is an exception) have started payments only at age six, or else have established ceilings on family totals.[82] In Africa, Kenya provides a flat transfer regardless of family size, while programs in Malawi, Ghana, and South Africa have capped benefits at four children.[83]

Financing

How much to transfer and to how many people depends to a large extent on what the government can afford. Middle-income countries are able to finance relatively generous cash transfer programs. The South African government spends between 11 and 12 percent of its budget, or about 3.5 percent of GDP, on social benefits that are distributed to more than 10 million children and 3.8 million old-age pensioners and disabled people.[84] Brazil's Bolsa Família and Mexico's Oportunidades absorb only 0.4 percent or so of GDP and cover almost a quarter of the population. The Bantuan Langsung Tunai unconditional cash transfer benefited a third of Indonesians for less than 1 percent of GDP.[85]

But what about poor countries? Although small budgets and weak administrative systems impose stark choices, social protection is possible. Benefits are often small, or limited to few beneficiaries. Nepal's universal old-age pension, for instance, costs about 0.1 percent of GDP, but only those older than seventy-five are eligible, and they receive the equivalent of $2 a month—about one-tenth of the per capita income.[86] Lesotho's universal Old Age Pension Program costs 1.4 percent of GDP.

Various simulations have estimated the cost of cash transfers in poor countries. Providing $1 a day to people older than sixty-five years in forty African countries would range from 0.1 percent of GDP in the Seychelles to a whopping 10.6 percent in Ethiopia, whereas transferring an amount equivalent to 70 percent of the national poverty line to the same age group in fifteen African countries would cost from 0.7 percent of GDP in Madagascar to 2.4 percent in Ethiopia.[87]

---

82. Handa and Davis (2006).
83. Handa and Davis (2012).
84. Authors' calculations based on data from the South African Treasury.
85. Grosh and others (2008).
86. Grosh and others (2008).
87. Grosh and others (2008).

According to the United Nations' International Labor Organization, some minimal level of social protection can be affordable even in poor countries. A universal old-age and disability pension set at 30 percent of income per capita and capped at $1 a day would cost between 0.6 and 1.5 percent of GDP in the twelve African and Asian countries the study considered.[88] A universal child benefit of 15 percent of GDP per capita for those less than fourteen years old would range between 1.2 percent of GDP for richer countries (such as India) and 3.6 percent for poorer ones (such as Tanzania), with costs diminishing over time in most countries. And providing some employment scheme for up to 100 days a year to those not receiving any other assistance would amount to 0.3–0.8 percent of GDP in those countries.[89]

One analysis of the fiscal space available for cash transfers concluded that countries should proceed with caution. The Overseas Development Institute (ODI) reviewed five African countries and found all were severely constrained, either by existing fiscal and macroeconomic restrictions or by limited administrative ability. In addition, the review warned that meeting targets for social spending would come at the expense of other sectors that might be contributing to economic development.[90]

Although scant resources are a significant challenge, poor countries that have adopted some form of cash transfer have demonstrated that minimum social protection is not a luxury only richer economies can afford. Some, such as Lesotho, dig into their own fiscal pockets. Bolivia and Mongolia have been taxing gas and mineral exports to help pay for cash transfers. And some countries, such as Ethiopia, have turned to foreign donors to help them foot the bill. That levels of social protection in low-income countries are not systematically related to per capita income suggests that fiscal constraints are only part of the story, and that politics are involved as well.[91] A study looking at the fiscal space for social protection in five countries in West and Central Africa concluded that small oil-rich countries in the Gulf of Guinea could afford both universal child benefits and social pensions, and also found space for more

---

88. These countries were Burkina Faso, Cameroon, Ethiopia, Guinea, Kenya, Senegal, Tanzania, Bangladesh, India, Nepal, Pakistan, and Vietnam.
89. ILO (2008).
90. DFID-UK (2011).
91. Kabeer (2009).

modest initiatives in the poorer countries.[92] The study concluded that developing political commitment, governance conditions, and administrative capacity was more challenging than finding budgetary resources in those countries.

Although countries can sometimes rely on external help in financing their social protection programs, it is not an ideal arrangement in the long run. Leaving governments out of cash transfer schemes often leads to small, fragmented programs that fail to capitalize on economies of scale, overlap, or are patchy, and leave beneficiaries subject to donor preferences and funding cycles. Yet only a third of the cash transfer schemes in sub-Saharan African countries are funded exclusively by those countries' governments.[93] In the poorest countries in the region, no program is financed by the public purse alone. Most initiatives are supported by a combination of government and foreign partners or exclusively by nongovernmental sources, such as donors or nonprofit organizations. The trend is shifting toward greater domestic funding and institutionalization, however. Some countries are seeking to reallocate funds. Ghana, for instance, is using resources from the Heavily Indebted Poor Countries initiative, started by the IMF and the World Bank in 1966, for its cash transfer program, and Malawi is relying on AIDS funds. Many countries could increase their tax collection to support cash transfer programs, and phasing out ineffective social programs would free up resources to finance more efficient cash transfer programs.[94]

The Politics of Cash Transfers

Cash transfer programs cannot take root unless political leaders champion them and convince middle-class and wealthy taxpayers that such programs represent money well spent, even though the money is not spent on those most taxed for them.

Attitudes toward poverty, and toward taxpayers' bearing some of the cost of relieving poverty, vary across countries. Taxpayers are more amenable to bearing the cost of social protection schemes if they believe

92. ODI and UNICEF (2009). The five countries were the Republic of Congo, Equatorial Guinea, Ghana, Mali, and Senegal.
93. Garcia and Moore (2012).
94. Garcia and Moore (2012).

that the poor deserve to be helped, that they will use the money wisely, and that giving them a hand does not make them dependent. This often takes some convincing. When Ghana launched the Livelihood Empowerment Against Poverty (LEAP) program to assist vulnerable children and orphans, the elderly, and the disabled, public concern centered not on the expense but on whether the money would be wasted by the poor. Ghanaian authorities launched a publicity campaign to explain the government's social protection strategy and the exact nature of the grants; the campaign was crucial to winning support for the program and ensuring its launch.[95]

Starting small and demonstrating positive results also wins support, paving the way for a wider rollout. Ghana's Ministry of Manpower, which championed the LEAP scheme, first secured relatively modest funds to develop and test its cash transfer program. It established a pilot program covering 1,200 people and designed with the experiences of Brazil, Zambia, and South Africa in mind. The initial pilot program helped convince the broader public of the benefits of cash transfers and nudged the Ministry of Finance to allocate money to expand the program.[96]

Monitoring existing programs helps not only to improve them but also to build support when positive results are widely shared. The popularity of Mexico's Oportunidades is attributed in part to well-documented evidence that the program eased poverty and encouraged recipients to send their children to school. In contrast, Nicaragua's Red de Protección Social illustrates that even successful programs cannot survive without sufficient popular support. Introduced in 2000 as a pilot project targeting the poorest families in six municipalities, the program increased nutrition, vaccination, and schooling while reducing poverty and child labor, all within two years.[97] Despite its success, however, the program was unable to mobilize political support, and its purpose and performance were misunderstood. There was no funding, and no time for a campaign to dispel the widely held view that the program bred dependency, trapped people in poverty, and cost too much. Administration of the program was transferred to the Ministry of the Family, which

95. Sultan and Schrofer (2008).
96. Sultan and Schrofer (2008).
97. Maluccio and others (2005).

meant a loss of autonomy, efficiency, and credibility. The program was discontinued in 2006.[98]

Implementation: The Mechanics of Cash Transfers

The most efficient programs make sure cash reaches the intended beneficiaries at the lowest possible cost while minimizing fraud and corruption. An increasing number of schemes are adopting electronic transfers and other innovative methods to distribute benefits: almost half of forty social transfer programs introduced since 2005 rely on electronic delivery of cash payments.[99] Even in the poorest countries, where the financial infrastructure is embryonic, innovation relying on mobile phones and card systems is taking root.

Electronic transfers tend to be cheaper, safer, and often more convenient. Recipients no longer have to travel to a specific location on a given day to collect their cash, which is instead deposited into a bank account. When Brazil's Bolsa Família switched its payment system to electronic benefits cards, administrative costs were slashed from almost 15 percent of grants to less than 3 percent. South Africa cut the costs of delivering its social security transfers by 62 percent when it started to use private bank accounts.[100] Electronic transfers are advancing financial inclusion in many countries, including South Africa, India, and Brazil, where more convenient and affordable financial products are now reaching even those without bank accounts. Where bank branches are unavailable or impractical, small shops or mobile phone networks can become service points. In addition, mobile phone networks are increasingly offering bankless payment systems, such as M-Pesa in Kenya.

Transferring benefits directly to recipients through debit cards or mobile phones also reduces opportunities for corruption, as officials—some of whom may be tempted to ask for bribes or pilfer straight from the till—are no longer needed to handle cash payments. And biometric data technology and personal identification numbers, which are gaining currency in the developing world, help weed out fraud.

The number and variety of cash transfer experiments currently under way and the growing popularity of these programs suggest that coun-

98. Moore (2009).
99. Pickens, Porteous, and Rotman (2009).
100. Pickens, Porteous, and Rotman (2009).

tries will continue to experiment with them. Because cash transfer programs lend themselves to experimental design and rigorous evaluation, they are also helping to create a new standard for impact. Increasingly, the question asked of development interventions will be, is this approach more effective than simply providing cash? This same question thus faces policymakers pondering how to spend a windfall: how might alternative expenditure options compare to cash transfers?

3

The Devil's Excrement?

"Ten years from now, twenty years from now, you will see: oil will bring us ruin. . . . Oil is the Devil's excrement."

—*Juan Pablo Pérez Alfonso, Venezuelan Minister of Mines and Hydrocarbons and architect of OPEC*

Of Africa's fifty-five countries, fifty are either producing or exploring for oil.[1] Yet in Africa as elsewhere, the potential of oil and other natural resources has been largely squandered.[2] Instead of delivering a better life for the poor, mineral wealth has time and again benefited an elite few, often with high economic and political costs. Oil and other natural resources are thought to fuel corruption, political repression, and even conflict, and an oil discovery is now often considered a curse rather than a blessing. This paradox is evident across regions, yet many natural resource producers have failed to take more than token steps to address it. The policy community similarly has many useful ideas to fight the resource curse, but these ideas have often made little difference to the final outcomes or have been swamped by countervailing pressures. Although the effects of sudden windfall gains have been studied and analyzed at length, effective solutions remain elusive.

In this chapter we examine the notion of the resource curse. Is it real? Why does natural resource wealth prove such a vexing problem for so many countries? What in the dynamics might suggest possible ways to mitigate—or even resolve—the challenges?

1. *The Economist*, "Show Us the Money," September 1–7, 2012.
2. Natural resource wealth comes in a variety of forms, including fossil fuels, rare metals, minerals, and timber. While we focus here largely on oil, the broader literature on the resource curse is relevant to other extractive resources.

Is the Resource Curse Real?

Since the 1980s, a growing body of literature has argued that natural resource wealth can hinder economic development. This argument appears counterintuitive—after all, one would expect countries endowed with natural wealth to benefit from their bountiful natural resources. Yet many resource-rich countries remain indisputably poor, conflict-ridden, and corrupt.

The "resource curse" remains a prolific if controversial research subject. Numerous studies have sought either to establish or to debunk theoretical and empirical links between natural resources and a host of negative outcomes: macroeconomic instability, export concentration, deindustrialization, high levels of poverty, rampant corruption, persistent authoritarianism, and a proclivity toward conflict. After more than thirty years of research, what do we know?

Economic Growth

The resource curse literature was in part born out of the observation that economies with abundant natural wealth seemed to grow not only slower than their wealth would predict but even more slowly than their resource-poor counterparts. In a seminal study, Jeffrey Sachs and Andrew Warner found that economic dependence on oil and minerals correlated with slower economic growth across 100 countries.[3] They argued that this paradox is not new: seventeenth-century Spain, for all its gold and silver from the New World, trailed the resource-poor Netherlands. In the last decades of the twentieth century, East Asian economic stars such as Singapore, Taiwan, and Korea far outshone oil-rich Venezuela and Nigeria.

Although several studies have confirmed Sachs and Warner's (1995) finding that natural wealth negatively affects economic growth,[4] others have found no evidence of such a link.[5] A recent study even found that

---

3. Sachs and Warner (1995) measured resource wealth by the ratio of natural resource exports to GDP, more accurately a measure of dependence. They controlled for the initial size of the economy, trade policy, investment rates, the volatility of terms of trade, inequality, and the effectiveness of the bureaucracy.

4. See Kaldor, Karl, and Said (2007), Ross (2001), and Sala-i-Martin and Subramanian (2003), among others.

5. See Brunnschweiler and Bulte (2006) and Stijns (2005).

oil had a positive effect on income per capita when regional dummies were added.[6]

These conflicting findings may reflect different definitions of natural resource wealth: are resource-rich economies those that enjoy an abundance of natural resources (measured, for instance, by natural capital per head) or those that depend the most heavily on it (measured by resource production as a percentage of GDP)? Scope—the sample of countries and the years covered—also influences results. Michael Ross examined fifty years of data and found that although economic growth in oil producers had been unusually erratic, over the long run it was neither slower nor faster than in nonoil producers.[7] This long-run "normal growth rate," Ross argues, raises a question: given their wealth of natural capital, why have oil producers failed to grow faster than average?

Drawing reliable conclusions from conflicting results is tricky, and cross-country studies that rely on large amounts of imperfect data should be viewed skeptically. Current-account statistics in poor countries are notoriously unreliable, and the relationship between national income and natural resource measures is problematic.[8] Given these constraints, the most relevant question may not be whether there is a discernible statistical impact on average but why some resource-rich countries develop successfully while others fail. Why, for instance, do Nigeria, Venezuela, and Angola appear to exemplify the resource curse,

6. Alexeev and Conrad (2009). See Frankel (2010) for a survey of the literature and a discussion of the competing econometric findings.

7. Ross (2012).

8. Since both measures of resource dependence (for instance, resource production as a percent of GDP) and resource abundance (natural capital per head) are at least partly endogenous to income, causal relationships between natural resources and income are hard (if not impossible) to establish. For instance, countries can be highly resource dependent because their poor business climate or protectionist government policies hinder the development of nonresource sectors. Poor growth can lead to higher resource dependence rather than resource dependence leading to poor growth. Similarly, measures of resource abundance are not fully exogenous either. Resource abundance is normally measured by proven (or probable) reserves, which, at least until recently, reflected domestic technological capacity to extract and explore for oil and minerals. Therefore, findings that resource wealth increases income could simply reflect the fact that richer countries are more likely to have the capacity to explore for and extract hydrocarbons (see Gelb, Tordo, and Halland [2014]).

while Botswana, Norway, and Chile appear to disprove it? Although geology is not necessarily destiny, it appears that under some circumstances, natural resources may threaten economic development.

Income Inequality

Even if resource-rich countries grow as fast—on average and over long horizons—as their resource-poor counterparts, that growth may not be distributed equally within the population. GDP growth rarely translates directly into higher incomes and a better standard of living for all citizens. In many resource-rich economies, it often does not translate into improved welfare at all.

There is evidence that the larger the share of commodity exports in a country's GDP, the more unequally income is likely to be distributed among the population.[9] There are plenty of rich oil-producing countries with poor populations. Oil has turned tiny Equatorial Guinea into the richest country in Africa, with a per capita income of more than $15,000 in 2011 (over $25,000 in purchasing power parity), yet more than three quarters of Equatoguineans remain poor. Similarly, Iraq is classified as an upper middle-income country, but nearly a quarter of its people live below the national poverty line.[10]

In some cases, inequality is widening. The wealthiest 2 percent of Nigerians collectively earned as much as the bottom 55 percent in 2000, compared to the bottom 17 percent in 1970. Almost 70 percent of Nigerians, who live in one of Africa's top oil-producing states, were trying to survive on less than $1 a day in the year 2000—a proportion almost twice as high as three decades earlier.[11]

Autocracy

As the world democratizes around them, oil producers account for an increasing proportion of autocratic states. In 1982, oil producers represented about a fifth of the world's autocratic states; two decades later,

9. Higgins and Williamson (1999); Gavin and Hausmann (1998). The impact of oil on inequality is difficult to study because inequality measures are hard to come by, particularly for oil producers. The higher a country's oil income, the less likely it is to disclose its inequality levels (Ross 2009).
10. West (2011).
11. Sala-i-Martin and Subramanian (2003).

that proportion had increased to more than a third. This trend has led many to wonder whether oil is bad for democracy.

Successful and durable transitions to democracy are rare in oil-producing states. Oil-rich countries are less prone to transition from autocracy to democracy: democratic transitions are about 50 percent more likely among nonoil states than among oil states.[12] And attempted shifts to democracy in poor countries have failed twice as frequently in oil producers, particularly in sub-Saharan Africa.[13] Although a rising national income usually facilitates democracy, the opposite appears to be true when the boost in income comes from oil.

The apparent negative influence of natural resources on democracy is, however, under scrutiny. Stephen Haber and Victor Menaldo looked at data over time rather than across countries and found that increases in natural resource dependence were not associated with either the undermining of democracy or poorer transitions to democracy.[14] Michael Ross and Jørgen Juel Andersen have challenged this finding, arguing that oil only began to hinder democracy after the 1970s as a wave of nationalizations allowed developing country governments to capture oil rents that foreign oil companies had previously captured.[15] This would explain why tracing the effects of oil on democracy back to the 1800s was inconclusive.

The debate over the connection between natural resource wealth and democracy remains unsettled. Ultimately, however, it raises a fundamental question about the impact of oil on the political dynamics of producing countries, and particularly how oil revenues insulate governments from public pressure. We explore this question below.

Corruption

When oil mixes with poor governance, it fills not only state coffers but also foreign bank accounts. Nigeria lost close to $400 billion to corruption between 1960 and 1999—enough dollar bills to cover the distance from Earth to the Moon seventy-five times. The former Nigerian leader General Sani Abacha alone is thought to have pocketed the equivalent

12. Ross (2012).
13. In middle- and high-income countries, on the other hand, oil seems to have little impact on democracy (Ross [2009]).
14. Haber and Menaldo (2011).
15. Andersen and Ross (2013); Ross (2012).

TABLE 3-1. **Performance of Countries by Budget Accountability Category**

Accountability category[a]	Oil producers	Mineral producers	Non-resource-dependent countries
Expenditure controls	22	52	48
Link policy, planning, and budget	17	37	35
Extrabudgetary operations	20	31	32

Source: Heuty and Carlitz (2009).

a. Scores are defined as an average of scores on questions of the Open Budget Index. A score of 100 represents a fully open budget (see www.openbudgetindex.org).

of 2–3 percent of his country's GDP for every year he was president.[16] Corruption is also rife in oil-rich Equatorial Guinea: the president's son, Teodorin Nguema Obiang, is suspected of funneling at least $75 million—nearly twice Equatorial Guinea's annual education budget—into the United States between 2005 and 2007 alone, most of which was deemed to have been the fruit of "extortion, theft of public funds, or other corrupt conduct."[17]

Fuels and minerals appear to breed corruption: all else being equal, and regardless of the region, a country with a higher share of fuel and mineral exports is likely to be more corrupt.[18] A 15 percent increase in the share of natural resources in the GDP translates into a worsening of Transparency International's Corruption Perceptions Index—which goes from zero to 10—by two points.[19] Oil producers are less likely to be transparent and accountable for their budgets (see table 3-1). And corruption undermines economic growth: by one estimate, if Venezuela were to reduce graft to the level of Chile, Chile to the level of the United States, and Kenya to the level of Taiwan, these countries' GDPs would grow by an extra 1.4 percentage points.[20] The impact of corruption on growth is particularly pronounced for less-developed economies. Unstable governments and weak institutions struggle to detect and punish graft, making it more likely that oil and mineral revenues will end up in overseas bank accounts rather than in local schools and hospitals.

16. Costa (2007).

17. Quoted in Ken Silverstein, "U.S. Government Documents Crime Spree by Dictator's Son: Why No Action by the Feds?," *Harper's Magazine*, November 16, 2009.

18. Leite and Weidmann (1999).

19. Gylfason (2001).

20. Leite and Wiedmann (1999).

Civil Conflict

Countries rich in oil and minerals also appear to be particularly susceptible to civil conflict. Diamonds and oil have financed brutal conflicts in
Sierra Leone and Angola, and the Democratic Republic of Congo, for all
its immense mineral wealth, seems mired in permanent strife.

The question of whether natural resources either cause civil wars or
prolong them has received much attention since the late 1990s. Paul
Collier and Anke Hoeffler originally concluded that dependence on natural resources—measured by the ratio of primary commodity export to
GDP—raises the risk and duration of civil war, up to a point.[21] Once primary exports are equivalent to about a quarter of GDP, the risk of conflict recedes. In other words, natural resources initially make war more
likely, until commodity wealth is sufficient to translate into a level of
military spending that discourages rebellion. Recent research seems to
confirm these findings, particularly with regard to oil. Since the early
1990s, oil-producing countries have been about 50 percent more likely
than nonproducers to experience civil war, and the risk of civil war more
than doubles for low- and middle-income countries.[22] As new low- and
middle-income countries join the ranks of oil producers, this is particularly worrisome.

However, the claim that natural resources fuel civil conflict has been
contested on several grounds. First, some studies find no link between
exports of primary commodities and the onset of civil conflict.[23] Second,
natural resource dependency and civil conflict may both be caused by
something else, such as a weak state. Third, instead of civil conflict flowing from resource dependence, the relationship may run in reverse: civil
conflict may drive out manufacturing and services, resulting in an
increased dependence on natural resources.[24] Angola's economy, for
example, was relatively diversified until civil war broke out in 1975. A
decade later, industrial output had dropped by almost half, and Angola
had become one of the most resource-dependent countries in the
world.[25] Finally, some studies have suggested that only onshore oil, gas,

21. Collier and Hoeffler (1998, 2002); Collier, Hoeffler, and Rohner (2006).
22. Ross (2012).
23. Fearon and Laitin (2003).
24. Brunnschweiler and Bulte (2008).
25. Ross (2004b).

and some lootable minerals (such as diamonds) are linked to the onset and duration of civil conflict.[26] Empirical analysis suggests that resources that are easily extracted and smuggled, such as diamonds or cocaine, are more amenable to rebel financing than resources such as timber or offshore oil.[27]

Even if there is a causal link between natural resource dependence and civil conflict, aggravating circumstances surely tighten the connection. Poverty, sluggish economic growth, ethnic and religious fragmentation, and a high proportion of young men within a country's population all play a part in fueling civil conflict.[28] This may help explain why the link between oil and violent conflict is weaker in Latin America: the region's lack of separatist pressures and politicized ethnic cleavages,[29] together with its higher income per capita, may partially shield it from the propensity for civil conflict that natural resource wealth may inflict on poorer, less stable regions.

Academics continue to debate the existence of the resource curse, and the question of the linkage between natural resource wealth and negative outcomes—poor economic growth, inequality, corruption, autocracy, and conflict—remains unsettled. However, for our purposes, we can draw two reasonably certain conclusions: first, there is something about oil and mineral revenues that produces negative economic and political outcomes in some countries, and second, resource wealth is not necessarily destiny.

Canada, the United States, the United Kingdom, and Norway are well-governed, prosperous oil producers. Chile and Botswana are by various measures among the most successful economies in Latin America and Africa, respectively, and both are highly specialized mineral producers. These successes, though, are few and far between, and most unfolded in countries that had relatively developed human and institutional capital long before revenues from natural resources started pouring in. Several oil-producing countries that are success stories had established strong constituencies for sound management, such as a business class or social groups with interests beyond resources, before the discoveries were made.

26. Ross (2004b); Fearon and Laitin (2003).
27. Ross (2004b).
28. Collier, Hoeffler, and Rohner (2006).
29. Sinnott, Nash, and de la Torre (2010).

However, for the many countries just discovering or beginning to produce oil, gas, and minerals—particularly those starting out with poor governance, limited constraints on the executive, and few other industries—the risk of the resource curse is all too real. The question is why countries with solid institutions have been able to catalyze resource wealth into economic prosperity, while so many others may end up wishing they had never won the oil lottery.

Dynamics of the Curse

What is it about natural resources that leads to so many negative economic and political outcomes, especially for poor and poorly governed countries? Extractive resources, particularly oil and minerals, with their high economic rents, are different from other industries: they are highly concentrated, have few linkages with the rest of the economy, are subject to unusually volatile prices, require relatively little labor, and generate fiscal revenues that accrue to the government directly, rather than indirectly through taxes levied on private sector income. All of these factors contribute to the economic and political/institutional mechanisms through which the resource curse operates.

Economic Mechanisms

Volatility. Extractive commodity prices are extremely volatile. Oil prices in particular are so fickle that models attempting to predict future prices do little better than a random walk.[30] When much of the economy and government budget is steeped in oil, price uncertainty makes economic management and planning particularly tricky, even for the most capable governments. For an oil exporter like Nigeria, the difference in production value with prices at $50 versus $150 a barrel is equivalent to a difference of 50 percent of GDP.[31] This uncertainty turns borrowing against future expected oil revenues—or even setting budgets on optimistic oil-price benchmarks—into a dangerous gamble.

Unless well managed, price volatility translates into wild fiscal swings for economies that rely heavily on commodity exports. To make matters worse, price volatility is often compounded, rather than counterbal-

---

30. The coefficient of variation of oil is 0.7; see Gelb (2010).
31. Gelb and Grasmann (2010).

anced, by fiscal policy. Governments find it easy to boost civil servant salaries and military spending when oil prices are high but much harder to rein in spending when prices fall. Nigeria, Venezuela, and Mexico, for instance, reacted to the oil bonanzas of the 1970s and early 1980s by spending faster than their economies expanded.[32] Despite the windfalls, their economic growth performance was dismal. During the 1973–81 boom, a typical capital-importing oil exporter ideally should have saved about 80 percent of extra revenues, yet most saved very little, or went on a spending spree.

Since revenues from natural resources flow first and foremost to governments rather than domestic firms and workers, this tendency toward profligate spending turns commodity price swings into booms and busts for the entire economy. Times of plenty when there is much to spend—and much to waste—alternate with rainy days of uncontrollable deficits and mounting public debt. The ensuing boom-bust cycle is extremely detrimental for the nonoil economy, making countries increasingly reliant on the primary commodity and therefore even more vulnerable to price volatility—a vicious cycle that is hard to break.

Except for a few countries such as Norway and Indonesia, most oil producers have been unable to protect their economies from the wild swings in oil prices. During the 1972–81 period, when oil prices skyrocketed following the 1973 OPEC embargo and the 1979 Iranian Revolution, oil exporters' economies grew by a disappointing 2.6 percent. This was slower than the average for middle-income countries over the same period and a slump from the 4.1 percent recorded for these same oil exporters over the 1965–72 period.[33] Unable to handle the price roller-coaster, oil economies have been bipolar over the past few decades, alternating spurts of moderate growth and prolonged stagnation or recession.

Besides hurting economic growth, these booms and busts also help explain why inequality thrives in oil- and mineral-rich countries. Macroeconomic volatility hurts people unevenly: the poor are often unable to hedge risks and end up poorer when times are tough; the well-off, on the other hand, have enough cushion to weather the crisis without major pains. Education widens the gap even further. When hard times hit, poor

32. Karl (1997).
33. Gelb and Grasmann (2010).

families often pull their children out of school, either because they need their labor or because school fees are unaffordable. But when the next boom comes around, these children do not return to school. During Mexico's 1995 recession, for instance, more than 5 percent of children aged twelve to twenty-five joined the labor force, which suggests that a number of them cut their studies short. But the economic recovery in 1996 did not reverse the flow.[34] When times are tough, children of wealthy parents, on the other hand, are likely to stay in school longer, until employment opportunities improve. The widening education gap that the commodities roller-coaster exacerbates is likely to entrench and worsen income inequality.

Dutch disease and export concentration. The mechanism most often blamed for the damaging impact of oil and minerals on economic welfare is the effect known as the Dutch disease. The term was coined in the 1970s in reference to the erosion of the Netherlands' manufacturing sector in the wake of rising costs fed by the inflow of gas resources from the North Sea.[35] More generally, "Dutch disease" refers to the risk that a sudden influx of foreign capital—resulting, for instance, from the discovery of natural resources—will lead to an appreciation of the real exchange rate. As a result, other exports become relatively more expensive and less competitive, struggle to attract capital, and ultimately decline. Countries are left increasingly dependent on their main resource export.

When there is little industry to speak of, the discovery of oil or other commodities does not appear to hurt other sectors. Equatorial Guinea is a case in point. When oil started flowing in 1992, manufacturing was largely nonexistent, and the production of cocoa, timber, and coffee, the country's traditional exports, had dwindled thanks to mismanagement and a shortage of labor; cocoa exports plummeted from nearly 40,000 tons in 1968 to 5,200 tons in 1980, while coffee and palm-oil production had almost vanished.[36] Consequently, the exchange rate appreciation and the shift of labor to the oil sector did not displace much other economic activity because there was very little to displace. Yet newfound natural resource wealth makes the emergence of other economic

34. Gelb and Grasmann (2010).
35. Gavin and Hausmann (1998).
36. Gelb, Tordo, and Halland (2014).

activities even more unlikely, condemning the economy to become and then remain concentrated.

Diversification—whether by protecting existing nonoil sectors or by pushing for new ones to develop—is indeed particularly hard for oil producers. Natural resources, and particularly extractive commodities like oil, gas, and minerals, are enclave sectors with few linkages to the rest of the economy. This means there are few opportunities to transfer technologies that could be useful in other sectors. Countries that produce toasters, for instance, can hope to eventually manufacture microwaves and refrigerators, as the technological leap from one product to the next is relatively short. But extractive technologies are harder to transfer.[37] Moreover, the ability to diversify depends in part on protecting nonresource sectors from swings in the exchange rate, which, as noted earlier, requires a fiscal discipline that is difficult to maintain under political pressure. Appreciating or volatile exchange rates can make nonresource exports uncompetitive, pushing investment into nontraded sectors.

As a result, few resource exporters successfully diversify: over the 1992–2005 period, oil and gas accounted on average for almost half of total fiscal revenues in thirty exporting countries.[38] In some cases the economic and fiscal dependence is far more severe: in Equatorial Guinea, oil generates about 90 percent of GDP, 98 percent of exports, and more than 90 percent of government revenues.[39]

While it may seem reasonable for resource producers to specialize in their primary commodity (where they have a strong comparative advantage), export concentration is risky.[40] Export concentration compounds the vulnerability of the economy to price shocks, particularly if the main export, such as oil, suffers from highly volatile prices. A drop in oil prices will affect a diversified economy like that of the United States much less than an oil-dependent economy like Gabon's. Diversification, in other words, is another way of mitigating price volatility. Moreover, with the exception of artisanal mining, hydrocarbon and mineral extraction usually provide few jobs.[41] For developing countries, diversifica-

37. Toto Same (2008).
38. See Gelb (2010).
39. Bornhorst, Gupta, and Thornton (2009).
40. Toto Same (2008).
41. For a more detailed exploration of the challenges and benefits of diversification for resource producers, see Gelb (2010).

tion is often desirable to promote more labor-intensive sectors that could absorb growing, underemployed populations.[42] Diversification can also protect economies against the risk of oil running out, or against technological shocks affecting demand. Ultimately, economies that fail to diversify have been shown to grow more slowly over the long term.[43]

Countries are not defenseless when faced with the Dutch disease, however. Remedies to encourage economic diversification include improving the business climate, removing barriers to foreign investment, adopting a careful monetary policy, or (somewhat more controversially) actively promoting certain industries. Indonesia, Malaysia, and Chile have successfully diversified their economies despite their mineral and oil wealth. Prudent spending to secure macroeconomic stability, a largely open trade policy, and investment of oil and mineral revenues in other export sectors have been credited for such success.[44]

Yet even countries determined to diversify rarely succeed. Sound policies, while essential, are not always enough: Botswana, despite having strong institutions and well-managed diamond wealth, has been struggling to develop a manufacturing industry, hampered in large part by geography. In addition, governments that can survive on resource rents alone may lack incentives to protect withering sectors or develop new ones, especially if they are nascent or lack powerful champions to advocate on their behalf. As Alan Gelb notes, "Many of the policy and institutional factors that enable countries to manage resource wealth well are equally important for their ability to diversify into other sectors."[45] To the extent that oil and resource dependence can have a detrimental effect on precisely these "institutional factors," however, natural resource production and export concentration can become a vicious cycle.

Potential resource depletion. Most other economic mechanisms that have been advanced to explain the resource curse do not appear to hold up under scrutiny. The Prebisch-Singer hypothesis that long-term commodity prices are on a secular downward trend (and therefore would

---

42. This is increasingly the case for more capital-intensive offshore drilling, which requires highly skilled, typically foreign labor. This labor is normally imported by foreign oil companies and offers few opportunities for low-skilled local residents.

43. See Gelb (2010).

44. Cavalcanti, Mohaddes, and Raissi (2012).

45. Gelb and Grasmann (2010).

constrain the economic growth of commodity exporters) turns out not to be supported by price data. Commodity prices appear to move more in irregular cycles, and various studies have found different long-term trends, depending on the years covered.[46]

Another concern is exhaustibility. Oil and mineral resources are non-renewable, and thus by definition are exhaustible. If countries are not investing every cent that comes out of the ground, they could be depleting national assets. What happens when resources run out? Recent research suggests that improvements in exploration and extraction technology mean that resources are not as exhaustible as they may appear when only current reserves are considered. The dynamics of discovery have so far shown that as production proceeds, national reserves have, perhaps counterintuitively, grown.[47] This suggests that geology is unlikely to put an end to the resource boom. The principal challenge is to invest current resource income in ways that provide long-term national benefits.

Political and Institutional Mechanisms

Economic prescriptions to mitigate the harm of oil and mineral production to macroeconomic stability and export concentration are well known. Adopting a prudent fiscal stance, however, is easier said than done, especially when the political economy of oil producers discourages such a stance. In fact, although the economic challenges associated with oil and mineral revenues should not be dismissed lightly, it is their impact on governance that most fundamentally threatens overall economic welfare.

Social contract: The tax connection. The more income oil produces, the less governments need to rely on taxes. Governments in oil-rich Algeria, Oman, Kuwait, and Iran derive 10 percent or less of their revenues from taxes on goods and services, compared to 25 percent or more in oil-poor Jordan, Lebanon, and Tunisia.[48] Taxes account for a paltry 2 percent of the Iraqi government's income.[49] On average, a one-percentage-point increase in oil revenue in relation to GDP is associated with a 0.2 percent reduction in nonoil revenues.[50]

---

46. Gelb (2010).
47. Gelb, Tordo, and Halland (2014).
48. Gelb, Kaiser, and Viñuela (2012).
49. Ross (2009).
50. West (2011).

Yet taxes can help make governments more accountable, more capable, and more responsive. In Western Europe and North America, but also in East Asian countries such as Taiwan and Korea, taxes have gone hand in hand with the emergence of accountable and effective states.[51] Taxation is at the root of a social contract that dates back to the rise of parliaments in Western Europe. Transferring greater rights to citizens and accepting greater accountability was the price that monarchs had to pay for the funds they needed to finance costly wars.[52] Slowly, the social contract evolved to what Mick Moore describes as "the exchange of tax revenues (for the state) for institutionalized influence over public policy (for citizens)."[53] Taxation promotes bargaining between the state and its citizens, as well as greater government accountability, transparency, and effectiveness.[54]

In many resource-rich countries, however, citizens lack this bargaining power. Even if citizens can monitor government spending, they often have little leverage to push for change. Put simply, governments that do not depend on citizens for funding do not need to pay attention to citizen demands. Taxation may be the best way of ensuring that governments act on behalf of the governed, and while it works imperfectly even in the most developed countries, it is likely better than the alternative.

Preliminary evidence from empirical analysis suggests that taxation is indeed associated with better governance. In a sample of 117 developed and developing countries, higher tax revenues as a percentage of GDP are correlated with better rule of law and bureaucracy and with less corruption.[55] A 2006 study using survey data from Benin, Cameroon, Ghana, Mali, and Mauritania confirmed that people often refused to pay taxes because they received few benefits in return.[56] Conversely, in Zambia and Tanzania, local governments that rely more heavily on local taxes devote a larger share of their budget to public services, while those that depend on central government transfers or foreign assistance spend relatively more on employee benefits and administrative costs.[57]

51. Bornhorst, Gupta, and Thornton (2009).
52. Moore (2007).
53. Tilly (1975); Bräutigam, Fjeldstat, and Moore (2008).
54. Moore (2008, p. 26).
55. Altunbas and Thornton (2011).
56. OECD (2008).
57. Hoffman and Gibson (2006).

Taxpayers usually want a say in how their money is spent. Empirical studies have confirmed that increased taxation, up to a certain point, results in citizens demanding good governance, and more intense citizen scrutiny results in more effective public spending.[58] In Argentina, for example, provincial governments that are most dependent on broad taxation have historically been the most democratic.[59] As Trevor Manuel, South Africa's former finance minister, has remarked, "When states are obliged to bargain with their citizens over taxation, or cannot rely on coercion or external resources, then they must become more responsive to their citizens."[60]

Governments that rely on taxation for revenue have a greater incentive to promote their national economies than governments that live off natural resource rents. When governments are funded by oil revenues, they can afford to be indifferent to the fate of nonoil sectors, but if their revenues are tied to the performance of the broader economy, fostering economic development becomes a matter of self-interest. More firms, more workers, and more foreign investors paying taxes all mean more money in government coffers. A government relying on taxes also has a strong interest in the prosperity of its citizens, as its own financial resources depend on it.

Without the accountability of the social contract—and the stronger bureaucracy and institutions that go with it—oil and mineral producers tend to squander windfall revenues. Free from citizen scrutiny, oil money tends to disappear into the black hole of government budgets, with little to show for it. There are many ways to spend badly, from corruption to bad investments, fuel subsidies, and inflated public employment. An ineffective bureaucracy and weak state institutions only make matters worse. As a result, the quality of public spending tends to plummet when spending soars, typically to levels of 40–50 percent of GDP.[61] During a previous oil boom, the faster that countries spent their oil money, the less effectively they governed.[62]

58. Devarajan and others (2011).

59. Gervasoni (2010).

60. Opening speech at the International Conference on Taxation, State-Building and Capacity Development in Africa, hosted by the South Africa Revenue Service. Cited in Everest-Phillips (2010).

61. Gelb and Grasmann (2010).

62. IMF (2007).

Nigeria illustrates how public spending can easily go to waste. Between 1973 and 1980—when oil prices skyrocketed—Nigeria's capital stock tripled. The public purse, swelling with oil money, was largely responsible for this massive investment: whereas the public sector accounted for about 20 percent of investment in the 1960s, it had ballooned to 55 percent by the end of the second oil shock.[63] Unfortunately, this investment did not pay off. Capacity utilization in manufacturing, which averaged 77 percent in 1975, dropped below 40 percent in the mid-1980s.[64] The construction of Nigeria's Ajaokuta steel complex, for instance, ate up billions of naira in the 1970s. More than thirty years after its completion, it remains a stillborn failure. Similarly, although 40 percent of Equatorial Guinea's public investment goes into infrastructure, most has been spent on public buildings and other prestige projects, with little productive or social impact.[65]

Transparency. Corruption festers in the dark; the less known about the public dime, the easier it is to divert it. Public finances in oil- and gas-producing countries are notoriously murky. An IMF study found that parliaments scrutinized oil windfall use in less than half of forty-four oil-producing countries, and transparency was a concern in about two-thirds of them.[66] About half of all of Azerbaijan's government spending, for instance, is channeled through the national oil company and falls outside the state budget.[67] Countries that rely heavily on oil and gas revenues perform particularly poorly in the Open Budget Survey, which measures budget transparency and accountability around the world. Many oil or gas producers provide little or no budget information, although Mexico, Colombia, and Indonesia—with scores twice as high as other oil and gas revenue–reliant countries—are notable exceptions. At the very bottom of the 100-point scale, Chad, Iraq, and Equatorial Guinea scored zero, while Saudi Arabia and Algeria scored 1.[68]

Political Pressure. By allowing governments to survive without taxes and operate in the dark, oil and mineral wealth weakens state institu-

---

63. Sala-i-Martin and Subramanian (2003).
64. Sala-i-Martin and Subramanian (2003).
65. Goldman (2011).
66. IMF (2005).
67. Ross (2009).
68. International Budget Partnership (2010).

tions. Weak institutions, in turn, struggle to spend their mineral wind-falls wisely, which makes fiscal discipline elusive.

Governing elites, powerful pressure groups, or even the population at large often attempt to capture a piece, or all, of oil and mineral revenues. When experiencing a windfall, countries with weak institutions and a fractionalized governing elite tend to squander what they gain—a phenomenon known as the "voracity effect"—as powerful rival groups appropriate extra revenues.[69] Government largesse during good times tends to benefit politically influential groups, such as civil servants and the military.[70] Oil windfalls in the mid-2000s, for instance, were used to boost public sector salaries in Algeria, Azerbaijan, Iraq, Nigeria, Trinidad and Tobago, Venezuela, and Yemen.[71] In Chile, 10 percent of the state copper company's exports are transferred to the military.[72] Powerful state-owned oil companies, such as Mexico's Pemex, also wield significant influence and often manage to extract substantial benefits from oil windfalls.[73]

When people know that they cannot trust their leaders to spend windfalls wisely in the future, they want to see benefits from the windfall immediately, through anything from subsidies to public employment and state contracts. For many, producing oil means that gasoline and other oil-derived consumption products should be cheap. This expectation leads to entrenched fuel subsidies. Yet energy subsidies are usually not money well spent. They favor those who consume more, who are typically the better off: in Ecuador, some 85 percent of the gasoline subsidy benefits the richest 20 percent.[74] Fuel subsidies also promote energy-intensive industries, which typically do not create many jobs. Subsidies also tend to leak to neighboring countries, as cheaper fuel gets smuggled across borders.

Once in place, fuel subsidies are difficult to eliminate. Attempts to do so have resulted in rioting in many countries, often leading governments to back down. When the Nigerian government attempted to scrap fuel subsidies in 2012, people took to the streets, worried not only that prices

69. Tornell and Lane (1999).
70. Medas and Zakharova (2009).
71. Medas and Zakharova (2009).
72. Webb (2009).
73. Webb (2009).
74. Sinnott, Nash, and de la Torre (2010).

would become unaffordable but also that the savings to the government purse would only line the pockets of corrupt politicians. So fuel subsidies typically remain in place, ballooning over time without responding to the fluctuations in oil prices. As a result, a number of countries in Latin America and Africa spend more on energy subsidies than on education.[75] By 2006, Yemen's fuel subsidy was larger than its entire budget for social services. The cost of subsidies is often hidden: in Nigeria, Bolivia, Algeria, and Azerbaijan, for instance, subsidies are financed directly from oil revenues or profits from oil companies and are not explicitly recorded in the national budget.[76]

Some countries, particularly in the Middle East, also spend their oil money on creating public jobs for their nationals: by the early 2000s, more than nine out of ten jobs in Kuwait were in the civil service.[77] And in Gulf countries, a public sector job usually means employment for life with generous benefits. As with subsidies, however, public sector employment becomes entrenched, resulting in a bloated bureaucracy that is difficult to trim when times are tough.

Even well-intentioned governments find it politically difficult to save windfalls when faced with acute poverty at home. Although Chile's decision to save its copper revenues proved to be a fiscal lifesaver when the 2008 crisis hit, it was an extremely unpopular move at the time. The Chilean finance minister, who opted to save rather than spend (and who is now regarded as a hero for his foresight), was Chile's most unpopular public figure at the time and was under intense pressure to spend the money.

For the less well intentioned, oil money buys political support, whether through patronage, corruption, or general largesse. This helps explain why oil-producing countries are less likely to become democracies. Oil autocrats, for instance, dispense higher gasoline subsidies than oil democrats.[78] Turkmens, who live under one of the most repressive regimes, get free electricity and cheap gas. This pork barrel largesse may be good for rulers keen to hang on to power, but it is bad for the economy. Without proper institutional checks and balances, resource booms provide politicians with the means to influence elections, mainly by pro-

---

75. Sinnott, Nash, and de la Torre (2010).
76. Medas and Zakharova (2009).
77. World Bank (2004).
78. Ross (2009).

viding public sector jobs in exchange for political support.[79] In a context of weak institutions, kleptocratic rulers use income from natural resources to divide and rule, buying off opponents and undermining the cooperation needed to depose them.[80] And for those not amenable to carrots, oil and minerals can finance sticks—or armies of sticks.

Wanting a bigger share of the oil pie may also fuel separatist tensions, as independence becomes a potentially attractive option for regions that sit on minerals.[81] Oil-producing regions often feel they get few benefits from oil extraction and in some cases, as in the Niger Delta, suffer heavy environmental consequences. Dispute over how to share oil wealth was a key factor in the war that pitted Sudan's north and south and eventually led to the country's split. Oil is also closely related to secessionist conflict in Angola's Cabinda, and is a source of tension for the Iraqi Kurds. "Finding oil," says writer Nicholas Shaxson, "is like dumping itching powder from helicopters, aggravating existing divisions."[82]

Traditional Advice to New Oil Producers

There are few effective prescriptions to ensure that new oil or mineral producers follow the path of, say, Botswana, and not Nigeria. General warnings about "wise revenue spending," "sound investment," and "avoiding corruption" are as vague as they are unhelpful. The few concrete pieces of consensus advice—to ring-fence oil revenues in a sovereign wealth fund and to adopt high standards of transparency—are good policies but do not address the underlying causes of the resource curse: the severance of the social contract between governments and citizens.

Ring-Fence Revenues

To address the challenges of managing oil windfalls, many countries have created special fiscal institutions to ring-fence, or set aside, oil revenues. Depending on their setup, these mechanisms can serve a number of purposes. Some stabilization funds are meant to smooth out boom-and-bust cycles by saving during times of plenty, when commodity prices rise above

79. Robinson, Torvik, and Verdier (2006).
80. Acemoglu, Robinson, and Verdier (2003).
81. Ross (2006).
82. Shaxson (2007, p. 230).

a set value, and by spending when the pendulum swings back. Other countries set up long-term sovereign wealth funds, which are government-owned investment funds, either to save national wealth for future generations or to hold money overseas to inoculate their economies against the Dutch disease. Some create funds to achieve all three goals.

Several sovereign wealth funds have successfully contributed to good resource revenue management. Norway pioneered the concept in 1990 with the creation of an account that receives all petroleum revenues, with the intention of saving part of the revenues to finance the pensions of its aging population. Today the Norwegian oil fund (officially the Government Pension Fund of Norway) is among the largest in the world. Similarly, savings accumulated during the copper revenue boom allowed Chile to weather the global financial crisis in 2008. These savings were used to finance a fiscal stimulus package and social spending—including one-off transfers to the poorest—when the economic storm hit, softening the blow and boosting the president's popularity.[83]

These fiscal arrangements have become popular. Of thirty-one oil producers in a 2007 IMF study, twenty-one had established stabilization funds.[84] Yet for all their popularity, stabilization funds are no guarantee that resource revenues will be better managed, and their performance has been mixed at best.

Funds are easy to create but hard to maintain. Price volatility, weak institutions, and political pressure to spend and capture oil wealth all conspire against fiscal rules. The experience of Nigeria's many funds, and more notoriously the Chad-Cameroon pipeline fiasco, illustrate that without a strong constituency with a stake in protecting the fund, narrow-sighted politicians can easily raid the savings. In 2003, Chad set up an internationally managed fund at a bank in London with strict allocation rules as part of the conditions of a World Bank loan to build a pipeline to transport oil. Soon after oil started flowing, Chad began to violate the World Bank's provisions, and eventually the arrangement broke down (see chapter 6). Nigeria has also established a number of funds and special accounts to hold oil savings, but they have served as little more than politicians' checkbooks. In the worst cases, special funds are not only ineffective at smoothing consumption, they are counterproductive, essentially

83. Sinnott, Nash, and de la Torre (2010).
84. IMF (2007).

passing on saved funds from responsible governments to their irresponsible successors. Even well-intentioned governments find that setting appropriate fiscal rules, structures, and reference prices is no easy task.

As a result, stabilization funds often succumb to rules that prove too rigid or to pressure to spend; some never even take off. Strict rules meant to shelter oil funds from arbitrary interventions seldom survive political pressures, policy shifts, or significant economic changes. Venezuela, for example, has changed the operating rules of its fund several times, and suspended its operation for a period in the year 2000 after a budget deficit forced it to turn to costly financing to cover mandatory fund contributions. Mexico's legislature authorized the depletion of its oil fund in 2002, Gabon has failed to fully abide by the rules it set for its own fund, and Ecuador and Papua New Guinea concluded that their funds were unworkable and scrapped them.[85]

Moreover, even well-functioning funds do not solve the problem of how governments use the revenues once they are funneled into the budget. Governments that continue to rely on resource revenues—even if they go through a stabilization fund—have little need to cater to their citizens' needs. Citizens, in turn, have no way of holding the government to account.

Without a powerful constituency to advocate for prudent fiscal management, stabilization funds and fiscal rules are empty shells that do little to ensure the proper management of natural resources. The IMF has found that oil funds and fiscal rules have no impact on a country's fiscal position and do not reduce the bond between spending and oil revenue.[86] This is not to say that countries should not adopt stabilization or sovereign wealth funds—in fact, a stabilization fund is crucial to prevent swings in oil prices from wreaking macroeconomic havoc and destroying the nonresource economy. However, a sovereign wealth fund alone will do little to ensure good resource-revenue management.

Be Transparent

Several initiatives try to shine a light into the black hole of oil and mineral revenues. The Extractive Industries Transparency Initiative (EITI),

85. IMF (2007).
86. IMF (2007).

a coalition of governments, companies, international organizations, and civil society, was launched in 2003 to coax oil and mineral companies to publish how much they pay, and governments what they receive. So far, fourteen countries, ranging from Norway to Nigeria, meet the transparency standards set by EITI, and another twenty-two are working toward meeting them. However, several major producers—including Sudan, Angola, and Venezuela, which are perceived as some of the most corrupt economies in the world—have refused to participate in EITI's voluntary efforts. Equatorial Guinea became a candidate country in 2007 but was booted out after it failed to make sufficient progress.

The Publish What You Pay network of civil society organizations has been pushing for more transparency in the natural resource sector. As a result of its work and new legislation included in the Dodd-Frank Wall Street reform act, oil, gas, and mining companies listed on the U.S. stock exchange will soon (legal challenges pending) have to publish all payments to foreign governments above $100,000. The European Union recently passed similar legislation. These initiatives signal a growing realization among both civil society and governments that opaque oil wealth presents a risk for all involved.

However, neither EITI nor the "publish what you pay" legislation addresses the demand side of transparency. Without a constituency willing to use this information to scrutinize the government and the power to bargain and hold the government to account, the information sits in reports gathering dust, and the outcome remains unchanged.

* * *

Although thirty years of research on natural resources have advanced our understanding of why certain countries struggle to turn natural resource wealth into improved welfare for their citizens, our practical advice to new oil and mineral producers hoping to avoid the resource curse remains incomplete. Adopting transparency measures and ring-fencing oil or mineral revenues in a sovereign wealth fund are partial steps that fail to address the debilitating impact these revenues can have on governance: the divorcing of the state from its social contract with citizens.

Without a powerful taxpaying constituency to scrutinize government spending and hold it to account, windfall revenues often do little to advance economic development. With large amounts of money extracted from the ground, governments have few incentives to build up nonoil sectors. This results in increasingly resource-dependent economies where the government controls a significant part of the revenues that natural wealth generates, often fueling rent-seeking, corruption, and, at times, conflict. Approaches that fail to address the fundamental political economy disruption between citizens and their governments in resource-rich states are ultimately destined to fail.

4

Designing and Implementing Oil-to-Cash

"I wanted to install a sense of ownership in all Alaskans that would incline them to support healthy resource development and resist unhealthy versions. . . . I wanted to pit collective greed against selective greed."

—Alaska governor Jay Hammond

Countries can sidestep the challenges associated with an oil bonanza by converting the revenue into regular income for their citizens through cash transfers. This is the Oil-to-Cash approach, and it is applicable to any windfall income. Thus, we could write about gas-to-cash (Timor-Leste, Mozambique), gold-to-cash (Zambia, Mongolia), ore-to-cash (Guinea), or even strategic-location-to-cash (Djibouti, Panama) programs. Regardless of the income source, the basic principles still apply.

This chapter lays out the three basic principles of Oil-to-Cash and considers key design options. It also explores the practicalities of implementing an Oil-to-Cash program.

The Three Steps of Oil-to-Cash

While the specifics of Oil-to-Cash may differ from country to country, the basic approach is grounded in three essential steps: create a dedicated fund to receive the revenues, establish clear rules for distributing dividends, and collect taxes on the dividends distributed.

Step One: Create a Separate Fund to Receive Windfall Revenues

Governments receiving oil or mineral revenues should first funnel most of these revenues, including signing bonuses, royalties, and other taxes, into a transparent and ring-fenced special fund. This initial receiving fund can serve multiple functions: it can promote transparency, serve as a mechanism for spending triage, and bring stability to inherently volatile oil revenues.

Transparency. A single catch-all fund that reports all inflows and outflows provides a point of focus for external scrutiny. Moreover, when revenues are channeled into a single, identifiable account, it is easier for citizens to monitor government decisions affecting oil revenues. With information in hand, citizens can then begin to ask questions. Are the oil contracts fair? Are correct amounts being dispersed to citizens? How much is actually coming into the account? Efforts by citizen groups and nongovernmental organizations to promote government accountability and transparency are often stymied by complex fund structures that mask different types of flows. A single, simple, open fund (ideally with some form of independent oversight) can bolster local efforts to promote better governance.

Spending triage. A single receiving fund also helps provide the clarity needed for informed and responsible downstream spending decisions: What are the country's spending options? How much should it allocate for current expenditures? How much should it save? How much should it distribute? How should funds be released to avoid stoking inflation or otherwise overheating the economy? How much should be allocated to special funds, perhaps for infrastructure, health, or education? How much should flow into the regular budget? By serving as a mechanism for spending triage, a single receiving fund can aid both the government's and the public's efforts to make clear, rational fiscal rules and allocation decisions.

Stabilization. By holding funds over multiple years and adhering strictly to fiscal rules, the fund can play a stabilizing role, counterbalancing the volatility of oil income. This is useful regardless of whether the income flows into the budget or directly to citizens, but it may be especially helpful in shielding the population from rapid fluctuations in prices and production. A stabilization fund is essential to help smooth the size of the transfers year to year.

As noted in chapter 3, simply creating a fund does not guarantee its success: funds often succumb to political expediency, bad management, or overly rigid rules. Successful funds share a politically powerful constituency vested in the fund's protection. Without this check on politicians or on immediate political pressures, oil funds can function more as checking accounts than as saving or stabilizing mechanisms. Linking dividends to the oil fund in a clear manner should give all citizens a vested interest not only in maintaining the fund but also in ensuring it is well managed.

Alaska's experience provides a useful example. After squandering its initial oil bonanza, the state established a sovereign wealth fund, the Alaska Permanent Fund, in 1976, backed by popular vote. The objective was to preserve part of the state's oil wealth for future generations. The Permanent Fund—now worth over $50 billion[1]—receives 25 percent of Alaskan oil revenues to invest in income-producing assets. Since 1982, the fund's dividend program has paid every Alaskan resident an annual cash payment linked to the earnings of the fund. The amount is calculated by taking half of the average net income earned on the fund's capital over the past five years and dividing it by the number of state residents. While the dividend itself is a nice bonus for each resident, its real impact has been to help protect the fund itself by creating a constituency with a strong interest in its survival and success. The popularity of the annual dividend has prevented the Permanent Fund from being raided by special interests, and the state legislature has even approved special contributions to the fund beyond what is constitutionally required. Some argue that the fund itself, despite the annual cash call on half its earnings, would not be as large as it is today without the dividend, or even that it would not have survived without the dividend.[2]

To protect their economies against wild swings in oil prices, political leaders in oil-producing countries must adopt behavior that is often anathema to oil-rich political dynamics: saving enough money when oil prices are high to cushion the fiscal downturn when they fall. To be clear, a medium-term receiving fund is a necessary component for Oil-to-Cash. A fully fledged sovereign wealth fund or another long-term savings or future generations fund are specific options that may complement this fund but are not strictly necessary (see chapter 3). The cash transfer programs in Timor-Leste, Mongolia, and Nigeria are described in box 4-1.

1. As of July 2014, it is the Alaska Permanent Fund Corporation.
2. Goldsmith (2012).

BOX 4-1. Special Funds: Experiences in Timor-Leste, Mongolia, and Nigeria

Timor-Leste created a fund and established a cash transfer program financed through its oil revenues, but the two are not closely connected. When Timor-Leste started collecting substantial oil revenues in 2005, political leaders decided that direct distribution would be a central plank of the allocation strategy. The government's revenues became several times larger than the country's entire preoil economy, and spending increased tenfold between 2004 and 2009.[1] In 2005 the government created a Petroleum Fund, which collects all oil revenues. Up to 3 percent of the net present value of the country's oil resources may be transferred to the budget in any year, but further withdrawals must be justified by the executive and approved by parliament. In 2008, Timor-Leste introduced an extensive cash transfer program, but the transfers are financed directly from the general budget.

Mongolia is also spending some of its oil wealth on cash transfers, and has created a special fund to do so. In 2008 the Mongolian parliament created a Human Development Fund to make every citizen of Mongolia, for the first time in the history of the country, equally eligible to own a share of the nation's mineral wealth. The fund's capital is derived from exploitation of the country's vast mineral wealth. A mechanism saves surplus revenue from mineral royalties when prices are high to compensate for later falling prices. The government did not initially establish the fund as an independent sovereign wealth fund but expected it to provide pension, health, housing, and educational benefits, as well as cash payouts. However, distributions amounted to 40 percent of the state budget in 2011, which fed 14 percent inflation and raised eyebrows at the World Bank and the IMF.[2] In 2012, Mongolia introduced a law to promote fiscal responsibility by limiting budget deficits to 2 percent of GDP, and soon after it began reforming the cash payouts from ad hoc payments to regular dividends. Whether these adjustments ultimately lead to a responsible fiscal framework that prevents the country's mineral wealth from wreaking macroeconomic havoc remains to be seen.

Nigeria established the Excess Crude Account (ECA) in 2004 to capture extra revenues in times of high oil prices and to stabilize the budget. The government set a reference oil price in the budget, and when prices rose above the reference price, the extra revenues were siphoned into the ECA, ostensibly to be saved for when prices fell below the reference price. By the end of 2005 the ECA had accumulated nearly $30 billion. About $12 billion of these funds were used in 2005 to buy back (at a substantial discount) all of Nigeria's outstanding debt owed to the Paris Club creditors. Beginning in 2007, however, when Nigeria's political leadership and economic management team changed, politicians raided the ECA, and it was almost wholly depleted by 2010.[3] Nigeria is now planning to try again: a proposed formal sovereign wealth fund will have a more autonomous governance structure designed to prevent or at least reduce pillaging. So far, there are no dividend proposals attached to either the ECA or the sovereign wealth fund.

1. Wallis, Gillies, and Akara (forthcoming).
2. Campi (2012).
3. IMF (2012b).

Step Two: Formulate Clear Rules for Universal, Regular, and Transparent Dividends Tied to Revenues

Once oil revenues start accruing to the fund, the government should distribute part or all of them to citizens according to the following principles:

Dividends should be equal and universal. Cash transfers from oil or mineral revenues are based on the principle that natural resources belong equally to all citizens, not just the political elites. They are a dividend meant to instill a sense of common ownership in the country's natural wealth. As such, payments should ideally be made in equal measure to all citizens, regardless of the specific location of the natural resources in the country. Distribution to all citizens, no matter where they live, creates a broad constituency invested in the program and its success. Alaska distributes dividends to nearly its entire population. To be eligible, applicants must simply be in good standing with the law, have been resident for one year, and intend to stay in Alaska.[3] In places where national identity is weak or has been damaged by civil war, a universal cash transfer could also help build a sense of common belonging, and thus serve as a mechanism for national unification rather than a source of friction. In most countries the ownership of natural wealth is already vested in the people by law, which lays the legal groundwork for universal dividends.

Dividends should be paid on a regular schedule. Oil-to-Cash transfers should be viewed as a right of citizenry, not as a gift from politicians. The frequency of transfers should not be left to the discretion of politicians but should instead occur on a predictable schedule. Beneficiaries are able to plan and optimize their spending only when they know in advance when they will be paid. This means that payments should be regular, whether they occur monthly, quarterly, or annually. Alaska pays out oil dividends once a year. Bolivia's original old-age pension payment was also disbursed once a year (on the recipient's birthday) but has recently moved to a monthly payment schedule.[4]

A regular payment schedule also helps make oil dividends an effective tool for monitoring the well-being of the stabilization fund. Comparing this year's or month's dividend against the last can prompt citizens to

3. Alaska Department of Revenue, Permanent Fund Dividend Division, Eligibility Requirements (http://pfd.alaska.gov/Eligibility/EligibilityRequirements).
4. Laserna (forthcoming).

ask specific questions about the fund's management. Is the dividend lower because of lower oil prices, or is money being diverted to other purposes? If so, how is it being spent?

Dividends should be calculated according to clear and transparent rules. The calculation of dividends should be easy to understand and well publicized, especially since cash payments are likely to fluctuate. The government should publicize total oil revenues received each year and should be transparent and straightforward in calculating citizen payments.[5] This approach enables beneficiaries to confirm that they are receiving the right amount, and will also minimize fraud. Beneficiaries of a cash transfer program in Mozambique, for example, often did not know how much they were entitled to and ended up receiving about two-thirds of what they could have.[6] Alaska, on the other hand, publishes the calculation of the annual dividend on its fund's website. Electronic payments with auditable trails can make the system even more transparent and minimize fraud, as discussed below.

Calculating dividends based on transparent rules also carries political benefits. First, it removes political discretion and thus reduces the risk that politicians treat the dividend as a gift to constituents. Instead, citizens are entitled to the dividend, and politicians have to make the case for collecting taxes. A clear rules-based system also reduces (though it does not eliminate) the risk that electoral populism will swamp the dividend, with political parties attempting to outbid each other with promises to raise the dividend in an unsustainable or irresponsible manner.

Dividend rules should be robustly tied to revenues. For Oil-to-Cash to work, the connection between the transfer and the underlying oil and mineral wealth must be iron-clad. Citizens must receive a share of the revenues, not an arbitrarily set (and fiscally unsustainable) handout. This means that the dividend payments should, to some extent, reflect production levels and prices. Maintaining that direct connection neutralizes the risk of governments promising ever-increasing payments divorced from their financing source that could become a political and fiscal liability. If production or prices decline, the dividends should

5. Several governments already publicize how much they receive from mineral and oil revenues through initiatives like EITI, which cross-checks government reports with payment reports from oil and mining companies.

6. Garcia and Moore (2012).

decline proportionally, so the fiscal purse is not left saddled with an unfunded cash transfer system.

Step Three: Use the Dividend Mechanism to Build Broad Tax Collection

Part of the distributed dividends should be taxed back to finance the government and pay for public services. This may seem inefficient: why distribute money, only to then take some of it back? The reasoning is that taxes create an essential bond between people and the state. Bargaining around taxes generates positive engagement between and among governments, citizens, and firms. Taxpayers have a good reason to hold their governments accountable. They want to know how their money is being spent, which promotes greater transparency. Governments that depend on tax revenue are in turn more likely to listen to their citizens than those that receive oil boons no matter what.

Taxing transfers is therefore an essential component of Oil-to-Cash. Transferring oil money directly to citizens encourages an Alaska-type scrutiny over the fund that delivers the dividends, but failing to tax part of it misses a fundamental opportunity to alter the relationship between citizens and their government. Cash transfer recipients will likely have some interest in wading through the often murky finances of their rulers to make sure they get their fair share. But a push for transparency and accountability with respect to all government revenues and spending is more likely to emerge if citizens pay taxes.

This opportunity has been missed in the few places that distribute part of their mineral and oil revenues straight to their citizens. They have chosen to distribute only a small percentage of their vast resource wealth, and instead of expanding the tax base to get some of it back, they reduce or forgo taxes altogether. There is currently no personal income tax in Bolivia, for instance, and the lion's share of fiscal revenues still comes from natural resource rents.[7] In 1980, Alaska's legislature abolished the state income tax. Jay Hammond, the former Alaska governor who presided over the creation of the state's Permanent Fund and failed to veto the income tax repeal, later reflected that "by repealing the income tax, . . . we reduced our means and severed the major constraint on runaway spending: the cord that attaches the public's purse to the fingers of politicians."

---

7. Laserna (forthcoming).

Taxing oil dividends may feel like a huge leap in countries where few people pay taxes and the government has little capacity to collect a broad tax. Fortunately, an Oil-to-Cash approach suits these environments. To implement a widespread transfer scheme, the government must create a national ID system, link each unique eligible individual to some kind of financial account, and be able to make payments into each account. Once in place, that same transfer infrastructure can form the backbone of a national tax collection system, with payments flowing in the opposite direction. Besides logistics, a common challenge for tax collection in economies with a large informal component is determining taxpayers' income. But starting out by taxing dividends circumvents this problem, as authorities know exactly how much has been transferred. In some countries the government may decide to begin with a transition period of withholding taxes on the dividend, both to give the tax authorities time to build a regular collection system and to introduce the population to the idea of paying taxes.

Design Options

The three steps outlined above—ring-fencing oil revenues, distributing dividends, and taxing those dividends—form the essential tenets of an Oil-to-Cash system. But how should such a system work in practice? There is no single approach appropriate to all, and programs should be designed to suit each country's political and economic landscape. A few questions must commonly be answered in designing such a program, however, and the design options tend to fall into one of a few groups (see table 4-1).

Conditionality

A first design question is whether cash transfers should be conditional or unconditional. Chapter 2 examined whether making cash transfers conditional on behavior—from schooling to clinic visits—improves outcomes. Whether it is the cash transfers or the program conditions that are ultimately responsible for improved enrollment or nutrition remains unclear. Furthermore, conditionality brings a range of practical challenges. Monitoring compliance is a difficult and costly endeavor for countries with weak administrations. Tying cash to conditions also means the government must be able to supply the services that beneficiaries are

TABLE 4-1. Summary of Cash Transfer Design Options

Type of transfer	Pros	Cons
Unconditional	Easiest and cheapest to administer; conditions not always necessary for behavior change	Fuels "welfare" arguments; politically difficult to achieve
Soft conditionality	Political signal; creates expectations; low administrative costs; behavior change still likely	Some abuse likely; could harm political consensus
Hard conditionality	Strong political signal; behavior change likely	Difficult and costly to enforce; undermines "universality"; may encourage cheating

required to use, or large segments of potential beneficiaries will be excluded. In addition, strict conditions often prove too onerous for the most marginalized recipients, resulting in their exclusion. More important, even if conditions are practicable, they would not be appropriate for an Oil-to-Cash dividend, which is premised on unconditional ownership of natural wealth and is not intended as social welfare.

Yet, regardless of whether conditions produce better outcomes, they may be politically useful in the early stages of a cash transfer program to help avoid objections that people are receiving handouts without doing anything in return. Virtually all programs, whether they impose conditions or not, have clear expectations about beneficiaries' responsibilities. A proposal for an Oil-to-Cash system in Venezuela found it politically necessary to tie the dividends to health and education expenditures.[8] Extensive conditionality and too much complexity, however, undermine the clarity of the system and its potential political appeal and impact.

Transfer Size, Calculation, and Frequency

How much of a country's oil or mineral wealth should be spent on cash transfers, and how much should people receive? In chapter 2 we pointed out that cash transfers that are too small fail to make any appreciable difference. But the opposite is also a problem: if transfers are too generous, they may discourage work, or introduce new inequalities and social tensions. In this case, limiting the amount of payments may make sense.

---

8. Rodriguez Sosa and Rodriguez Pardo (2012). See chapter 7 for a more detailed description of the Venezuelan proposal.

Timor-Leste's $8,500 one-off payments made to protesting soldiers, for instance, reflected the soldiers' potential for destabilization rather than their need, and fed a sentiment that they had been rewarded for causing trouble. The lowest veteran pension of $276 a month is many times higher than the average Timorese income and a fortune for the 50 percent or so of the population thought to be surviving on less than $1.25 a day. The larger pensions, which can be as much as $750 a month, place recipients among the highest earners in the country.[9]

The simple solution to overly large transfers is to cap payments. Most Latin American countries, for instance, have set transfers at about 20 percent of the poverty line. To address potential concerns about population growth, many child grant programs have also set per family caps.

How often should payments be made? The relationship between the frequency of payment and how the additional income is used remains unclear. Studies in India suggest that more frequent—monthly or weekly—payments are largely spent on food consumption and schooling;[10] while in Mexico, bimonthly payments help households save more and invest in productive assets.[11] Payment frequency often depends on what is operationally feasible, however. More frequent payments are administratively more challenging and potentially costlier, as in Bolivia, when old-age pensions moved from an annual to a monthly payment schedule.[12] At the same time, an annual payment, if transferred to all recipients on the same date, may fuel chunky consumption patterns.

Degree of Universality

Although natural resource wealth should ideally be shared among all citizens, absolute universality is not feasible everywhere. In a country where a distribution to every citizen would put too much pressure on the public purse or reduce the transfer to a meaningless amount, choices about eligibility or targeting may be necessary.

When funding is limited, it is tempting to channel it to those who need it most. Such targeted transfers make sense as social welfare, but

9. Wallis, Gillies, and Akara (forthcoming).
10. Banerjee and Mullainathan (2010).
11. Gertler, Martinez, and Rubio-Codina (2006).
12. Laserna (forthcoming).

not under the premise that natural resources belong to all citizens. In any case, transferring cash only to the poor requires a sophisticated bureaucracy and enforcement mechanisms absent in most oil producers. So if oil or mineral revenues are not sufficient to fund a meaningful distribution to everyone, they should be targeted to easily identifiable demographic groups, such as the elderly or children. A focus on these groups may also be an implicit way of targeting the poor without means testing. This approach still respects the principle of universality in that everyone will benefit from the program at one point in his or her lifetime. It is also cheaper, simpler, and easier to administer.

Bolivia, for instance, has been using part of the revenues from natural gas exports to expand a program supporting the elderly that began in 1997. Renta Dignidad benefits citizens sixty years old and older, and its funding includes about a quarter of the national direct tax on hydrocarbons. By 2009 the program was covering more than 750,000 people.[13]

The principle of equal and universal payments does not dispute the reality that local communities close to the point of extraction may face environmental or economic challenges (such as spoiled fishing grounds or oil leaks) that might warrant special compensatory payments. But these payments should be separate, in calculation and mechanism, from the Oil-to-Cash dividend. The idea of weighting dividends based on proximity to production may be politically popular in some quarters, but drawing boundaries that can easily become flashpoints is politically dangerous.

Similarly, restricting cash benefits to a few selected groups based on other criteria can have significant negative aspects and be highly risky, particularly when objectives are confused or eligibility can itself become a source of conflict. Timor-Leste started distributing part of its oil revenues through cash transfers in 2008, primarily to veterans of the twenty-four-year struggle for independence from Indonesia. At the same time, one-off cash grants were made to a group of disgruntled soldiers known as "petitioners," others to the elderly, and yet another program targeted vulnerable, low-income households headed by women. In other words, cash transfers have been used to promote stability but also to offer social protection, combining short-term considerations with long-term objectives.

---

13. Laserna (forthcoming).

Payments to veterans and soldiers, however, have been subject to escalating demands, leading to expanded eligibility criteria and a ballooning financial bill. The veteran program transferred $18.8 million to just under 4,000 recipients in 2008. By 2010 it was distributing over $45 million to almost 9,000 people. Cash transfers to veterans alone were estimated to have consumed more than 10 percent of the country's entire budget in 2011. The targeting of veterans led to escalating demands for compensation by the excluded groups, with rapidly rising costs and heightened social tensions—a perfect example of the risks inherent in targeting groups, and why an Oil-to-Cash system should be as universal as possible.

Part or All of Revenues?

How much of oil or mineral revenues should be dedicated to cash transfers? The smaller the share, the more likely the government will be able to avoid levying taxes and continue to exhibit rentier behavior. Experience in Alaska and Bolivia suggests that governments should bind themselves by giving up enough direct income that they are motivated to collect taxes. As already noted, collecting taxes is both administratively and politically costly; governments that give up just 10 percent of their revenues are therefore unlikely to embark on a tax-collection project. Governments that give up a larger share, on the other hand, will have a greater incentive to recoup some revenues by taxing recipients. Starved of easy oil money, governments would have to rely on taxation to fund their spending. Yet political reality makes it unlikely that a new cash transfer program could absorb the majority of oil or mineral resources at the expense of government coffers.

Bolivia allocates about a quarter of the national direct tax on hydrocarbons to bankroll the Renta Dignidad program.[14] The Alaska Permanent Fund absorbs 25 percent of the state's direct oil revenues as capital, and the annual dividend transferred to Alaskans is paid out of 50 percent of the income generated by that capital, averaged over five years. The Permanent Fund has averaged a return of 8.7 percent over its lifetime and generated $35 billion in income, about half of which has been distributed to Alaskans.[15]

14. Laserna (forthcoming).
15. Goldsmith (2012).

Implementation

Once questions of design are settled, how can a country actually implement an Oil-to-Cash system? While the details of any oil dividend program must be tailored to individual country contexts, four components are required for any system to work: a public information campaign to explain the program, reliable identification of citizens, electronic mechanisms to transfer funds, and a system for taxing back some of the dividends. Fortunately, recent technological advances make these components increasingly feasible and affordable.

Public Information Campaign

To work, Oil-to-Cash must be clearly explained to the public and transparently executed. Oil-to-Cash transfers should be carefully presented not as a government handout but as a way for citizens to reap their rightful share of the country's oil wealth.

Potential beneficiaries who are unfamiliar with cash transfers may not understand the Oil-to-Cash concept immediately. Many people want to benefit from oil and mineral wealth but believe the only way to do so is through public investment. In Bolivia, for instance, the poorest initially rejected the idea of direct distribution. They argued that revenues should be spent on schools, hospitals, and roads, even though they blamed corrupt politicians and inefficient bureaucrats for squandering the country's natural wealth. They warmed to the idea of direct distribution only once it had been publicly debated and explained.[16] Similarly, the vast majority of Mongolians originally seemed to favor in-kind benefits over cash.[17]

Once the concept is understood, clearly communicating the logistics of the program is essential to its success. How much will be distributed, and to whom? When and how will these distributions take place? Data on coverage, audits, and program evaluations should be available at the very least on request, but preferably through broad public information campaigns on radio, billboards, posters, and even through SMS messages. Namibia, for example, launched an awareness campaign to improve coverage of its underutilized grant program, and announces

---

16. Laserna (forthcoming).
17. Campi (2012).

FIGURE 4-1. Mama Liberia: Taxation as Development

payment days on the radio.[18] Lesotho publicly posts lists of beneficiaries.[19] In Kenya, meetings are organized in targeted areas, and information is available through a website, pamphlets, and posters.[20] Liberia has embarked on a large-scale "Mama Liberia" public awareness campaign via posters to promote the idea of paying taxes (see figure 4-1). In Ethiopia, 90 percent of beneficiaries who felt they had enough information were satisfied with the program, compared to 75 percent of those who did not.[21]

One option is to distribute cards that explained the concept with simple math. Figure 4-2 shows an example of what a promotional information

18. Cited in Garcia and Moore (2012).
19. Cited in Garcia and Moore (2012).
20. Cited in Garcia and Moore (2012).
21. Cited in Garcia and Moore (2012).

FIGURE 4-2. Prototype Dividend Card

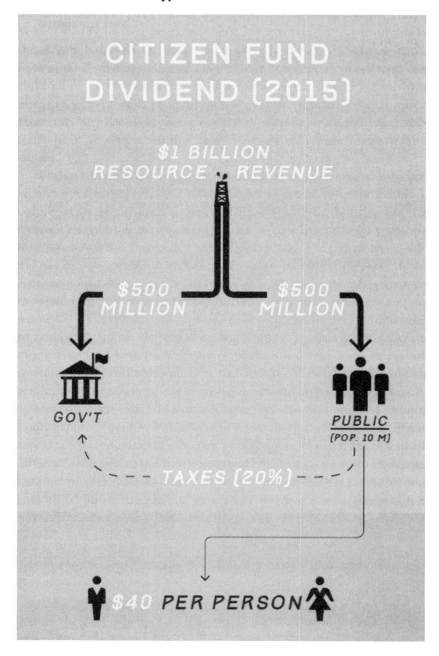

card might look like, explaining the calculations behind the dividend citizens are receiving.

Identifying Citizens: Biometric IDs

Successfully distributing cash to a large number of people, let alone a country's entire population, requires minimizing opportunities for fraud and corruption. Most developing countries lack reliable systems of identification: some have ad hoc identifiers or incomplete birth registries, while others have no system at all. A key precursor to implementing a universal system of transfers is to roll out an identification system that can identify citizens for payment and prevent abuse. Unique identifiers, particularly new biometric identifiers, can help prevent payments to ghost citizens and noncitizens and double payments. While many cash transfer programs have relied on more traditional identification systems, the growing access to and declining cost of biometric identification make it increasingly feasible, even for the poorest countries.

Biometric identifiers are "any automatically measurable, robust and distinctive physical characteristic . . . that can be used to identify an individual or verify the claimed identify of an individual."[22] In addition to fingerprints, biometric records may include face prints, iris scans, and even voice prints, retinal scans, tongue prints, and lip movement recognition. Identification techniques based on biometric characteristics are useful to ensure that an individual has not already registered and to authenticate someone against a record to confirm identity, enrollment, or eligibility.

Biometric identification has become widespread in both developing and developed nations. Recent studies estimate that more than 1 billion people in developing countries have had their biometric data recorded, including almost 300 million Africans and more than 400 million South Asians.[23] This number is expected to keep growing over the next five years. While many of these programs are small, India's current attempt to enroll its entire population demonstrates that biometric identification on a massive scale is indeed possible. As of 2014, India's Unique Identification Authority had enrolled more than 750 million Indians in a system that records all ten fingerprints and both irises. If India, with

22. Woodward, Orlans, and Higgins (2003).
23. Gelb and Clark (2013).

its 1.2 billion citizens, can register its entire population biometrically, most other countries should be able to learn from its experience and follow suit. Biometric identifiers have been used to support cash transfers in places such as the Democratic Republic of Congo and emergency relief in Pakistan after the floods.

How accurate are biometric identifiers, and what are the risks associated with inaccuracy? The experience of many biometric programs demonstrates that the risks of both false negatives (failure to identify that a person has already registered) and false positives (incorrectly recognizing a person who has not yet enrolled), while real, can be minimized. By harnessing the combined power of two identifiers (fingerprints and iris scans), India's Unique Identification program reduced the probability of a both a false negative and a false positive to well below 1 percent in a sample of 84 million.[24] Some individuals may have biometric identifiers that are hard to capture, such as worn fingerprints from a life of hard agricultural labor, which may prevent them from enrolling and lead to exclusion. However, the use of multiple biometric identifiers should mitigate this risk, as those with worn fingerprints may resort to iris scans. The more dangerous risk of exclusion is through explicit discrimination that formally marginalizes undocumented individuals. This is a risk not inherent in biometrics, however, but more generally tied to identification systems.

Is biometric identification too costly? Although the equipment required for biometric enrollment has indeed been expensive, costs are falling significantly. The cost of enrollment in developing countries now averages about $5 per registrant, and in India it is about $3 per registrant.[25] Although the cost of an entire biometric enrollment process can be steep, having one secure identification system is certainly more cost-effective than having to improvise systems of identification each time a new intervention is rolled out. Moreover, savings from the prevented fraud and leakage (such as funds lost through corruption or high transaction costs) can in the long term more than make up for any up-front costs. In Nigeria, biometric audits reduced the number of federal pensions by almost 40 percent (from 97,000 to 60,000).[26] The savings were equally impressive in Botswana ($1.7 million, or a 25 percent drop in

24. Gelb and Clark (2013).
25. Gelb and Clark (2013).
26. Gelb and Decker (2011).

registrations), and in the Indian state of Andhra Pradesh, with a 12 percent drop in recipients. So far, biometric identifiers have been used to support cash transfer programs in about a dozen countries, successfully reducing fraudulent registrations (and therefore leakage) wherever implemented.

Transferring Funds through Electronic Payment and Mobile Banking

Government-to-person payments have traditionally been made by handing out physical cash in person, an approach that is both costly and prone to leakage. Moving truckloads of cash around the country is neither efficient nor safe. The current revolution in electronic and mobile payments, however, is changing how people transfer money to each other even in the poorest countries. Governments can take advantage of these new technologies to deliver oil dividends at minimum cost and with very little leakage, while simultaneously helping to extend access to financial services to the poorest.

Electronic payments can be deposited straight into bank accounts or handed out as debit cards. New branchless banking technology opens the door for wider coverage of areas underserved by the traditional financial sector. Where the banking system fails to provide universal coverage, the network of mobile prepaid card vendors usually does. With new mobile financial services, governments can deposit money directly into citizens' cellphone accounts.

A well-known example of mobile money transfer is M-Pesa in Kenya. As of late 2011, M-Pesa served over 15 million customers in Kenya alone (more than 60 percent of Kenya's adult population), had a network of more than 45,000 agents, and transferred approximately U.S. $700 million each month in person-to-person transactions.[27] Over the past few years, M-Pesa has spread to other African countries, including South Africa and Tanzania, and as far as India and Afghanistan. Although M-Pesa remains by far the most successful platform, it has inspired the launch of numerous other mobile money systems. There were already 150 live mobile money systems and 110 planned ones across seventy-two developing countries in 2011, according to GSMA's mobile money tracker.[28] If necessary, initial oil dividends could even be transferred in the form of a low-cost handset.

27. Chandy, Dervis, and Rocker (2012).
28. Chandy, Dervis, and Rocker (2012).

About half of social transfer programs launched over the past decade feature some type of electronic payment.[29] Whatever form it takes, electronic delivery can slash the administrative costs of a transfer and leave an auditable trail all the way from the issuer to the final recipient—a powerful tool to minimize corruption.

Taxing Back a Portion of the Dividends

Expanding and improving tax administration in poor countries—let alone building one from scratch—is challenging, to say the least. It is difficult and costly to collect taxes from low-income farmers or informal urban workers. Taxable units are small, income is variable or seasonal, the cost of collection is high, and records are nonexistent. Tax collection is carried out face-to-face, and often the same person is charged with assessing and collecting payments—a system that generates incentives for collusion and opportunities for corruption.[30] Without the ability to enforce, tax evasion becomes the norm. All of these factors make governments more likely to focus their efforts on a few large taxpayers (such as foreign corporations) and to rely on indirect taxes rather than a broad tax base, which is good for minimizing the cost of collection but poor for governance.

How can governments build a tax system to collect back oil revenues? Perhaps the easiest option is to withhold taxes from the dividend payments. Just as payroll taxes are withheld in most developed countries, governments could announce a gross dividend payment, withhold taxes, and actually transfer to citizens the dividend net of taxes. However, the potential drawbacks of this seemingly simple approach should be weighed against the efficiency gains. First, it remains unclear whether this "virtual taxation" would generate the governance impact of actual tax payment. Citizens may accept the net payment as given and ignore the taxes, potentially undermining the governance effects. Second, it would not automatically broaden the tax base beyond the withheld dividend. This would largely depend on whether governments chose to recover the fiscal revenues that were distributed by extending the scope and reach of the rest of the tax system.

Another option is to institute a system of sales taxes, like a value-added tax (VAT), which may be relatively easy to enforce and collect.

29. Pickens, Porteous, and Rotman (2009).
30. OECD (2008).

However, whether VATs are a good replacement for direct taxes remains contentious. On the one hand, they are less likely to discourage work and savings than income taxes, and they tend to be relatively simple to administer and comply with. On the other hand, because the poor spend disproportionate amounts of their income on consumption, VATs could be regressive if not carefully designed.[31] Finally, and most worryingly for an Oil-to-Cash system, VATs are indirect, and thus may not be visible enough to generate political mobilization. Citizens may see an increase in prices but not feel as though they were being taxed, which undermines incentives for bargaining and citizen oversight of revenue spending.[32] Excise taxes on products like tobacco and gasoline can also raise revenue and prevent negative externalities (from health risks and pollution) but are vulnerable to smuggling and illicit production.

A third option is to roll out a comprehensive tax system. The systems that a government must put in place for Oil-to-Cash transfers—notably the identification system and associated financial plumbing—could in fact provide a platform for expanding the tax base. For its Oil-to-Cash program, the government would have identified all citizens and established a pipeline linking each individual to a financial account. To collect taxes, the funds would have to flow the opposite way—from individual to government, rather than from government to individual.

In most countries, this approach would complement and significantly enhance existing tax collection. Countries would still have to strike a balance between direct (corporate and personal income taxes) and indirect taxes (such as sales and excise taxes). On paper, most developing countries already have income taxes, but in practice they are collected on a narrow tax base and yield very little revenue. Estimates suggest that only 5 percent of the population in developing countries pay personal income tax (compared to 50 percent in developed countries), and only 15 percent of taxable income is reached.[33] For governance benefits,

---

31. See IMF (2011). There is significant debate about whether VATs are necessarily regressive or whether there are certain design options (such as high thresholds for mandatory reporting or an exemption for basic foodstuffs) that might mitigate their regressive tendency.

32. Whether indirect taxes like VATs are less likely to generate positive governance benefits is debated. Von Soest (2008) argues that VATs have been highly visible in Ghana and Uganda, generating controversy and suggesting a direct effect in bargaining between governments and citizens.

33. IMF (2011).

it is not necessary for every single citizen to immediately begin filing and paying income tax. Taxpayers in the early European systems were originally a small group of wealthy landowners and only slowly evolved to include the wider population. Similarly, developing countries could slowly expand their personal and corporate income tax collection from the current narrow bases, first to include civil servants, waged employees, and larger companies, and then slowly broaden toward including the full population and small businesses.

While tax reform is never easy, it is possible. Over the past decade Tanzania has instituted a series of major reforms to address its low revenue collection, including increasing the capacity of the revenue authority, rationalizing the small taxpayer administration, and substantially simplifying personal and corporate income taxes. Altogether these reforms steadily raised taxed revenue from 9 percent of GDP in 2000 to 15.3 percent in 2009. El Salvador, Vietnam, and Mozambique all adopted similar policies and capacity-building reforms over the past decade, successfully raising their tax revenue-to-GDP ratios by three, four, and seven percentage points, respectively (see box 4-2).[34]

A country's strategy for expanding the tax base to collect part of the distributed oil revenues should be guided by its administrative capacity, the structure of its economy (that is, how agrarian it is), and political considerations. However, initially withholding dividend payments while slowly building capacity to tax a broader cross section of personal and corporate income can generate immediate revenue and promote accountability and oversight as direct taxation eventually expands. Everyone can contribute to the government through the withheld tax on the dividend, and as incomes rise (and processes for accessing nondividend income taxes improve), citizens will be incorporated into a broader tax system.

34. See IMF (2011). The figures for Mozambique are for non-resource-related tax revenue.

BOX 4-2. Mozambique's Tax Reform

In 1992, shortly after the end of its devastating civil war, Mozambique embarked on an ambitious reform of its tax system and administration. The sixteen-year civil war decimated the Mozambican economy and the government's ability to raise taxes. Between 1981 and 1985, real GDP fell by around 25 percent, servicing external debt represented over 200 percent of exports, and the formal economy collapsed to less than a third of GDP. Partly as a result of the war, during which large areas were outside government control, revenue collection was extremely weak, limited to a few geographic areas, and plagued by corruption.

After the civil war ended, the economy started recovering and the government began modernizing the tax system. Reform was rolled out in two stages. The first stage, from 1994 to 2000, focused on reforming indirect taxes by replacing cascading taxes with a VAT and certain excise taxes, and restructuring the VAT and customs administrations. The second stage then tackled direct taxation, and culminated in the creation of the Mozambique Revenue Authority, with jurisdiction over both customs and domestic taxes. Together, the two phases of the tax reform yielded impressive improvements across four areas:

—*Collections.* Tax collections increased from 8.7 percent of GDP in 1993 to 16.2 percent by 2009. Tax evasion and noncompliance also declined significantly, with collections increasing from 51 percent of total potential revenues in 2002 to 66 percent in 2007.

—*Equity.* The adoption of a personal income tax improved tax equity. Yet the large number of microenterprises that operate outside the tax system points to a substantial remaining equity gap, as relatively few taxpayers shoulder the bulk of the tax burden.

—*Economic efficiency.* Reducing custom tariffs, replacing the sales taxes with a VAT, and merging the multiplicity of corporate tax rates into a single corporate tax rate removed distortions and helped direct investment toward more efficient sectors.

—*Corruption.* Reforms allowed the tax authorities to reclaim control over tax collections and reduced the proliferation of different regulatory and legal standards. This included the development of professional career paths for staff, the adoption of ethics codes, and the creation of internal audit units with broad powers to investigate corruption. The granting of tax exemptions, however, continues to present opportunities for wrongdoing and leaves room for improvement.

Source: Castro and others (2009).

5

Gauging the Benefits of Oil-to-Cash

"Asked what's the maximum benefit they've received from oil, no doubt most [citizens] would say dividends."

—Alaska governor Jay Hammond

Why is distributing oil or mineral revenues directly to citizens better than the alternatives? What are the benefits of Oil-to-Cash? In brief, depriving governments of easy oil revenues and forcing them to bargain with citizens to collect taxes can deliver significant economic and political benefits, as well as other, indirect benefits. We touched on many of these benefits in earlier chapters; here we explore their different dimensions in greater detail.

Economic Benefits

Among the principal economic benefits of Oil-to-Cash are macroeconomic stability, improvements in the immediate welfare of recipients, and efficiency gains. Oil-to-Cash can also enhance the government's interest in broader economic growth and capture welfare gains by shifting spending to private consumption, and can have a positive multiplier effect on internal markets.

Macroeconomic Stability

Regardless of how they ultimately spend their oil revenues, all oil producers need to find a way to protect their economies from wild swings in oil prices. This necessity will inevitably require setting up some kind of stabilization fund that captures excess windfall when prices are high to smooth the fiscal contraction when prices fall. As evidenced by the failed attempts described in chapter 3, however, setting up sovereign wealth funds is often the easy part. Without a powerful political constituency to protect them, oil funds are vulnerable to being raided by myopic politicians and powerful special interest groups who benefit from spending but gain little from saving. To the extent that an oil dividend program guarantees the integrity of the fund by giving each citizen a stake in its success, it can foster macroeconomic stability—an important prerequisite for diversifying the economy and achieving a more broad-based economic prosperity.

Tangible Welfare Benefits

Evidence from Latin American cash transfer programs suggests that distributing oil revenues to people does more to help the poorest citizens than almost anything else the government might do with the money. Cash transfer programs are among the most rigorously studied social interventions, and their development impact has been impressive.

Among other things, regular Oil-to-Cash dividends could do the following:

Significantly dent or eradicate extreme poverty. Distributing Equatorial Guinea's oil revenues would amount to more than $10,000 per citizen each year. As three quarters of Equatoguineans currently live on less than $2 a day, the distribution of even a small fraction of this amount could eradicate poverty in Equatorial Guinea. A recent study estimates that by distributing the revenues just from production increases, Iraq could halve poverty within two to three years.[1] Nations with abundant natural resources relative to their population size and with an ineffective public administration could significantly reduce poverty by transferring less than 10 percent of their oil income to citizens.[2]

Build human capital. Cash transfers have been linked to positive education and health outcomes for children, which can help break the intergenerational transmission of poverty. South Africa's Child Support Grant, for instance, has led to improved school attendance, particularly

1. West (2011).
2. Devarajan and Giugale (2013).

among children who live with their mothers, while children in households that receive pensions in Lesotho attend school more regularly and are better fed than similarly situated children in families that do not receive pensions. Mexico's Oportunidades raised the height-for-age of beneficiary children by 1 cm after two years, while in South Africa a child receiving the Child Support Grant in early childhood is predicted to gain an average of 3.5 cm in height as an adult as a result of improved nutrition.[3]

Build local markets and invest in productive enterprises. Evidence from cash transfer programs suggests that most of the money is spent locally. Local sellers and producers benefit from the increased demand, which generates positive multiplier effects throughout the local economy. Cash transfers in Zambia, Namibia, and Lesotho, for example, have stimulated local businesses, and a study of a cash transfer program in Malawi found a multiplier effect of two kwacha for each kwacha disbursed.[4] While most of the cash in transfer programs is spent on food, a small but significant part is usually invested, possibly in part because predictable incomes allow the poor to take risks on small enterprises. In Ethiopia, 15 percent of participants in a cash transfer program invested in farming and 8 percent purchased livestock. In Paraguay, beneficiaries invested almost 50 percent more in farming, while 12 percent of transfers in Mexico were invested in productive activities, with return rates averaging 18 percent.[5]

Economic Efficiency Relative to Subsidies and Other Indirect Distribution

Cash transfers are one of several ways countries can choose to share their resource wealth. The political reality of oil economies means that the real choice is not between distributing rents or not distributing rents but between doing so directly (through transfers) or indirectly (through subsidies, artificially low taxes, and excess public employment). Most governments choose the indirect path, passing on part of oil revenues to citizens through subsidies and lower or no taxes. While subsidies are one way of distributing oil revenues to citizens, they are almost always inefficient, regressive, highly distortionary, and expensive. Benefits, even

3. Evidence compiled in DFID's Cash Transfer metastudy (2011). For a more detailed analysis, see chapter 2.
4. Davies and Davey (2007).
5. DFID-UK (2011). See chapter 2 for more detailed evidence.

when they are supposed to help the poor, usually are quickly captured by elites. In addition, subsidies are extremely difficult to reverse once in place. Any reduction in subsidies is met with fierce resistance that in some cases has threatened or toppled governments.

Unlike subsidies, universal cash transfers are neither distortionary nor regressive. They help the poor manage food price hikes without distorting the market prices of fuel or energy. And because they make up a significantly higher percentage of income for the most deprived, they are more progressive than subsidies or tax cuts. Cash transfers can be engineered to be less expensive than subsidies and, as in Alaska, to smooth out short-term commodity price swings.

Government Incentives Aligned with Broader Economic Growth

Oil-rich governments receive a paycheck from oil companies regardless of the state of their economies or the welfare of their citizens. Their paycheck depends almost exclusively on oil production, international oil prices, and their ability to hide, not reveal, the true inflows to the country. Redistributing oil rents to citizens and forcing the government to rely on taxes—both corporate and personal income taxes—functions like performance pay: it ties the fortune of government revenue to the broader welfare of the economy. Without oil funds to boost their coffers, governments should have stronger incentives to adopt policies that support all sectors to maximize their tax revenue. A booming economy will boost revenues, while stagnation in nonoil sectors would have a negative impact on government coffers. Thus, by aligning the interests of the government with greater economic productivity, a system of taxed cash transfers could boost household incomes and fiscal revenues without sheltering the government from the dangers of neglecting the welfare of the economy at large.

Countries with abundant natural resource revenues face diminishing returns to public spending and benefit from transferring some of the revenues to citizens for private consumption. In countries where natural resource wealth is substantial relative to the size of the population and the public sector is inefficient, transferring some of the public rents for private consumption and investment is likely to be more economically efficient.[6]

6. Devarajan and Giugale (2013).

Political Benefits

Along with its economic benefits, Oil-to-Cash has distinct political advantages. Experience suggests that Oil-to-Cash can boost government accountability, support national unity, and help build bureaucratic capacity, all of which have wider positive repercussions.

Enhanced Accountability

Oil-to-Cash can help build accountability in two ways. First, such a program provides an oversight mechanism by which citizens can monitor the source of oil dividends (normally the oil fund). Second, it promotes broader government accountability through taxation and the social contract.

As we noted in chapter 4, cash transfers from natural resource revenues give citizens strong incentives to monitor financial flows in and out of the stabilization or sovereign wealth fund. Because citizens would have a direct personal stake in the resource wealth, cash transfers would likely motivate recipients to protect the integrity of the fund.

But Oil-to-Cash promotes accountability on a larger scale as well. By taxing the cash transfers—the final step in an Oil-to-Cash program—governments will ultimately come to depend on tax revenues and be forced to build a tax administration, rather than bypass constituents by relying solely on rents. Creating incentives to build and broaden the tax base in this way is perhaps the most important potential benefit of Oil-to-Cash. Citizens would become far less likely to remain passive recipients of government largess and instead would become potentially active contributors, while also demanding that the government be more responsive to their needs in return for their taxes (see box 5-1).[7]

These different accountability effects—oil revenue oversight and expanded taxation—are complementary. The latter requires transferring sufficient amounts of money to citizens to incentivize governments to tax. Transferring just 10 percent of revenues may not do the trick; governments may prefer to rely on the remaining funds, as Alaska did, rather than go through the effort of taxing it back.The former could work with small transfers, as in Alaska's program, but may not be sufficient to alter the relationship between the citizens and the state unless

---

7. For evidence on the connection between taxation and accountability, see chapter 2, box 2-1.

BOX 5-1. **Empirical Evidence of a Social Contract**

Although the idea of a social contract between government and those governed is grounded in the historical analysis of the evolution of European parliaments, more recent studies have sought empirical evidence for the link between taxes and accountability:

—*Cross-country studies.* Large-sample-size studies have shown that higher tax revenues are associated with better governance and increased scrutiny of government spending decisions, particularly for direct forms of taxation, such as income tax, that have a more noticeable impact on voters' wallets.[1] Another study looked at public perception polls and found that an abundance of natural resources decreases perceived tax enforcement, which in turn decreases demand for free and fair elections.[2]

—*Subnational variation.* New literature on the relationship between tax dependence and governance compares subnational governments within the same country. A study of Argentina found that provinces most dependent on broad taxation of their citizens had historically been more democratic than those more dependent on central transfers or oil revenues.[3] Similarly, a 2009 study found that as local taxes increased, district governments in Tanzania and Zambia devoted a larger share of their budget to public services, whereas those dependent on central transfers tended to spend more money on bloated bureaucracies and public servant benefits.[4] A third study found that areas of Nigeria where the British built local tax collection capacity today have local governments with higher levels of public approval, better public service delivery, and lower levels of corruption than areas where the British failed to build up those institutions.[5]

—*Experimental.* An experiment conducted in resource-rich Indonesia found that both transparency and taxation strengthened the propensity of citizens to demand good government.[6] More recently, a series of experiments in Uganda found that taxation led citizens to demand more from leaders by activating a "stronger fairness norm," which was particularly pronounced for those with more experience paying taxes.[7]

---

1. Bräutigam (2008b).
2. McGuirk (2010).
3. Gervasoni (2006, 2011).
4. Hoffman and Gibson (2006); Berger (2009).
5. Berger (2009).
6. Paler (forthcoming).
7. Martin (2013).

---

taxes are introduced. Citizens may be keen to monitor the fund from which their dividend is paid to ensure it is properly managed, but they may not extend the scrutiny to other government spending.

National Unity

A universal dividend can promote cohesion in countries where oil revenues would otherwise be more likely used to promote one group over another and generate conflict for control over rents. Oil dividends can help prevent conflict and bolster peace in oil-producing states.

Since about 1990, low- and middle-income oil producers have been twice as likely as nonproducers to experience civil wars.[8] Giving each citizen an equal share of oil revenues removes a large source of grievances, the unequal distribution of rents. Moreover, taking away government discretionary control over how mineral wealth is spent also makes it less attractive to control government and thus could, in theory, lessen incentives to rebel. Cash transfers may also prevent conflict by raising incomes and thus the opportunity cost of joining a rebellion: when people have more to lose, whether in income or business, they are less likely to take up arms. Transfers also give rebellious or violent groups a direct stake in keeping the production of natural resources peaceful and raise the cost of insurgent activity, as disruption of oil pipelines by disaffected groups affects the dividends of the entire nation, including those perpetrating the violence.

In addition, cash transfers in countries emerging from war provide tangible benefits in remaining part of the state and accepting the new political order. In other words, transfers can help secure a peace deal by ensuring buy-in from rebel groups. Cash transfers funded by oil revenues targeted at veterans and internally displaced persons in Timor-Leste were aimed at creating postconflict stability by co-opting potential sources of renewed violence.[9] Recently, a similar proposal for oil dividends in Iraq was partly based on the premise that it could quell some of the sectarian violence.[10] Biometrically linked cash transfers have been used as part of disarmament, demobilization, and reintegration programs in such places as the Democratic Republic of Congo. Payments were distributed to combatants who disarmed, to encourage them to keep the peace.[11]

The conflict angle is a critical rationale for why the dividends should be as universal as possible. If there are segmented benefits or regional disparities in eligibility, the definitions themselves could become sources of conflict, especially if eligibility became hotly contested.

Strengthened Bureaucratic Capacity

Taxation is central to state building, both because of the social contract created by bargaining around taxes and because of the need for capable

8. Ross (2012, p. 145).
9 .Wallis and others (forthcoming).
10. West (2011).
11. Gelb and Decker (2011, p. 17).

institutions.[12] The need to raise revenue to fight wars in Europe led not only to greater citizen rights and the rise of parliaments but also to effective and professional state bureaucracies. Shifts from tax farming—whereby taxes are collected by private sector collectors in exchange for a fee—to more permanent bureaucracies made tax collection more predictable and less predatory, while the growing demand for literate and numerate bureaucrats underpinned the growth of formal education systems. Parliamentary demands for the reports and information needed to hold monarchs accountable and support legislative proposals led to a further demand for more skilled and sophisticated bureaucracies.

This bureaucratic capacity has benefits for the rest of the economy. The process of collecting information about producers and basic data on the economy, setting fiscal priorities, establishing effective regulation for the private sectors, and fostering the adoption of modern accounting builds the bureaucratic and technical capacity of the state, which also improves the provision of public services.

Indirect Benefits

The above economic and political benefits of Oil-to-Cash flow directly from the model itself. There are, however, indirect benefits that countries can also reap. These indirect benefits may not be what spur a country to adopt an Oil-to-Cash approach to managing a natural resource windfall in the first place, but they can be valuable secondary benefits worth considering.

Development of a National Identification System

Beyond its use for distributing oil dividends, a biometric system of identification has several ancillary development benefits, as described below.[13]

Identification in its own right. Lack of official documentation can severely limit opportunities for economic, social, and political development. Official IDs are often necessary to vote, gain access to public services, register property, or open a bank account.[14] The "identity gap" in developing countries is large: UNICEF estimated that in 2000, some 40 percent of children in the developing world were not

12. Bräutigam (2008).
13. Gelb and Clark (2013).
14. Gelb and Clark (2013, p. 1).

registered at birth.[15] Lack of identification also predominantly affects the poor, making development less inclusive. While biometrics are not necessary for national identification systems (the United States relies on driver's licenses and Social Security numbers), they are helpful in protecting against fraud.

Public service delivery. Biometrics have been used extensively to improve service delivery, particularly in health care. Many programs use biometrics to verify program eligibility, including insurance, and to limit fraud by ensuring that benefits are not stolen or transferred to the wrong people. Biometrics have also been incorporated into health systems to help store patient data and track hospital visits or specific courses of treatment. They are used, for example, to ensure that patients do not miss second doses of vaccines and to track adherence to antiretroviral treatments for HIV/AIDS.

Civil service reform. A growing number of countries use biometric technology to reduce fraud in paying public servants, as well as to monitor job attendance. Nigeria's Integrated Personnel and Information System, for instance, claims to have eliminated 43,000 ghost workers as of July 2011, while smaller Guinea-Bissau's biometric census of civil servants cut 4,000 ghost workers from the public service payroll.[16] In parts of India, biometric readers have also been used to reduce teacher absenteeism and to monitor civil servant attendance.

Voter rolls. At least thirty-four low- and middle-income countries have incorporated biometric technology into their electoral processes to limit fraud. The technology first ensures that citizens register only once to vote, and then verifies that those who vote are actually registered. Because of the time constraints around elections, establishing a biometric voter roll from scratch often runs into logistical and resource constraints. Slowly rolling out a biometric identification system as part of a dividend program and then extending its use to electoral rolls may be the best way to take advantage of the technology. This approach would prevent electoral fraud, and would also moot the scramble to install a sophisticated and large-scale identification system a few weeks before an election.

Emergency response. Biometric identification can significantly help governments respond to emergencies such as earthquakes and floods,

15. Cited in Gelb and Clark (2013, p.7).
16. Gelb and Clark (2013, p. 28).

when paper documents are particularly likely to be lost. Pakistan's Watan program provided reconstruction grants to more than 1.5 million families affected by flooding, using a national biometric database. Leakage was minimal, and the estimated travel cost of withdrawing the money was around 1.4 percent of the grant amount.[17]

Secure financial services. Relatively simple fingerprint technology has been used for more than two decades to authenticate financial transactions. Recently, more precise digital biometric technology has been adopted in such places as Bolivia, Mozambique, Nepal, and Nigeria. Accounts are often linked to smartcards that are at biometric ATMs. This helps poorer, rural, and illiterate people access banking services. Biometrics can also help banks fulfill their "know your customer" requirements. In India, for example, the Unique ID numbers are accepted as proof of address and valid identification for banking purposes. Biometrics combined with mobile money have also enabled the creation of "biometric money"—or secure, cashless transactions.[18] Ghana and Liberia are two countries linking biometrics with a civil servant payroll to deposit money directly into bank accounts, helping minimize corruption and weed out ghost workers.

Financial Access

Two to three billion adults worldwide are unbanked or underbanked. Fewer than one in five sub-Saharan Africans have a bank account, while in Asia the figure ranges from 40 percent to 60 percent.[19] Paying dividends to entire segments of the population in developing countries will probably require setting up a significant number of either formal bank accounts or virtual mobile money accounts for citizens who lack them. When Iran replaced its fuel subsidies with cash payments, 16 million new bank accounts were opened for previously unbanked citizens.[20] In and of itself, improved access to financial services (facilitated by identification from a biometric or other secure identification system) can have a significant positive impact on the welfare and development prospects of the poor.

As David Roodman notes in his book *Due Diligence,* poor people living on $2 dollars a day do not actually earn $2 dollars each day; they

17. Gelb and Clark (2013).
18. Ibid.
19. Karlan and Morduch (2009).
20. Guillaume and others (2011).

often earn $4 one day and $0 the next. Managing this kind of income volatility makes putting food on the table each day difficult for people without access to basic financial services. Savings kept under the mattress are vulnerable. Savings are so important to the poor that, unlike the rich, who demand a return for their savings, the poor are often willing to pay a premium for a safe place to hold their extra cash and an external binding mechanism to compel them to save. Women in a southeastern Indian village, for example, were willing to pay up to 30 percent of their savings for someone to collect a small amount each day, forcing them to put money aside.[21] Saving systems allow the poor to add up small, uncertain income into larger amounts to pay for investments like school fees, or to insure against shocks from illness.

Providing citizens with a bank account as part of an oil dividend program can help households manage their income volatility through savings, rather than having to borrow at steep interest rates from moneylenders once a crisis hits. In Bumala, Kenya, a local village bank offered free savings accounts to randomly selected micro-entrepreneurs, such as vendors or bicycle taxi drivers. Within six months, women who opened an account had invested more in their business, increased personal spending from 68 to 96 cents per day, and increased food spending from $2.80 to $3.40.[22] This small experiment suggests that giving people access to savings accounts can significantly improve their welfare.

* * *

Oil-to-Cash programs, if properly designed and executed, offer resource-rich countries the potential to effectively manage economic volatility, assist the poor, nudge governments toward better economic management, transparency and accountability, and bolster national cohesion. Through the use of biometrics and electronic transfers, they can also advance financial inclusion and a proper identification system, while taxation carries the seeds of improved public administration. Too good to be true? Impossible? In the next chapter we address the understandable skepticism directed at Oil-to-Cash.

21. Roodman (2012, pp. 30–31).
22. Dupas and Robison (2009).

6

Oil-to-Cash Won't Work Here!
Answers to Ten Common Objections

"When I am getting ready to reason with a man, I spend one-third of my time thinking about myself and what I am going to say and two-thirds about him and what he is going to say."

—Abraham Lincoln

When policymakers and other interested parties talk about Oil-to-Cash, they tend to voice a predictable set of doubts. These criticisms often focus on claims of better uses for the money, unforeseen consequences of a dividend, or some unique logistical or political barrier in a particular country. In this chapter we respond to the ten most serious objections to Oil-to-Cash, largely by drawing on the arguments and evidence presented in earlier chapters. For many, the response is a plausible counterfactual (how do cash transfers compare to the alternative policy options?), a clearer articulation of the available evidence, or ways for real worries to be mitigated through smart program design.

1. We Can't Give Income Away Directly to People When My Country Needs Roads, Hospitals, and Power Plants

In theory, spending new revenues on public investment is a wise choice. To be sure, the supply of infrastructure in most developing countries is far from adequate and severely handicaps businesses: few serviceable roads and a lack of dependable electricity mean farmers cannot get their goods to the market, while factories must install costly generators or risk frequent blackouts.[1] In low-income, capital-constrained countries,

1. The World Bank's Enterprise Surveys suggest that 40 percent of firms in developing countries see electricity supply as a major constraint to doing business, with

deficiencies in infrastructure reduce productivity, and ameliorating them could yield large returns.[2]

Using oil revenues to overcome these obstacles and help build up the nonoil economy appears to make sense—if only those investments translated into usable roads and functional electric grids. Unfortunately, there is little reason to assume that public investment will be highly productive.[3] Worse, the track record of government investment in infrastructure is notoriously bleak.

Infrastructure in low-income countries has historically been prone to project selection problems and corruption. Roads are more likely to be built to the president's village than to the port; white elephant projects (with expected kickbacks) are likely to be built at the expense of more urgent investments. Côte d'Ivoire, for instance, boasts the largest church in the world (whose construction carried a hefty price tag of $300 million) in the impoverished and sparsely populated capital city of Yamoussoukro, where few households have access to running water and adequate sanitation.[4]

Even if priorities are in the right place, large-scale construction has been among the sectors most susceptible to corruption.[5] Rough estimates suggest that anywhere from 5 percent to 20 percent of construction costs are lost in bribe payments alone, which could amount to $18 billion a year in developing countries.[6] Yet bribe payments represent only one of the many costs of corruption. Much worse than a 10 percent markup in the cost of building a bridge because of kickbacks is corrupt officials subtracting 10 percent from the budget, resulting in a poorly built bridge that collapses within a few years. The total economic impact of corruption that results in poor-quality construction and skewed spending priorities is likely to be substantially higher than the cost of the

---

each firm experiencing an average of nine power outages a month; almost one in three firms own a generator to provide backup power or as their main source of electricity (see Kenny [2011]).

2. Dabla-Norris and others (2011).

3. Pritchett (2000) has argued that the idea that public investment is equal to capital accumulation is a heroic assumption because public investment is not inherently productive.

4. Foster and Briceno-Garmendia (2010).

5. Kenny (2007).

6. Kenny (2006).

bribes.[7] This means that the real cost of corruption in infrastructure far exceeds the 5–20 percent estimates. This does not set a particularly high bar for cash transfers to beat.

Not only is public infrastructure investment notoriously inefficient, oil producers are particularly bad at it compared to nonproducers. An IMF index on the efficiency of public investment finds many current oil exporters trailing at the bottom quartile of the rankings.[8] Oil producers are also significantly less transparent about their budgets and rank lower on measures of budget accountability, according to the Open Budget Index (see table 3-1).[9]

Moreover, investment in infrastructure or other sectors does nothing to address the effect of oil on political institutions and the social contract. Already poor public sector productivity is likely to worsen as the state becomes even more divorced from the population and from public accountability. As resource rents increase, so too may the incentives for civil servants and politicians to engage in patronage, rent-seeking, and corruption.[10]

So, while low-income countries are undoubtedly in need of roads and hospitals, it is not at all evident that oil rents should be primarily funneled into infrastructure projects. In countries where it is already clear that public expenditure suffers from low efficiency and high levels of corruption, a major injection of new funds should be weighed against other options according to the likely impact and use of those funds in practice, not in the mere hope that such funds could be theoretically used well *if* the system improved.

2. Any New Income Would Be Better Spent on Bolstering Depleted Social Services

As with infrastructure, pouring oil money into social services works better in theory than in practice. To be certain, health and education services are inadequate in many low-income countries. However, health

7. Kenny (2006).
8. Dabla-Norris and others (2011).
9. Bornhorst, Gupta, and Thornton (2009); Bird, Martinez-Vasquez, and Torgler (2008); Devarajan and others (2011).
10. Gelb (1988); Karl (1997).

and education ministries and systems are plagued by corruption and inefficiencies, and often are unable to transform increased funds into improved social outcomes.

Growing evidence points to high levels of leakage and extremely low levels of service delivery for the supposed beneficiaries in many of the new oil producers. Some two dozen public expenditure tracking surveys have been conducted in developing countries, mostly in sub-Saharan Africa.[11] The first of these, a 1996 study in Uganda, showed that 87 percent of nonwage education spending was lost before reaching the schools for which it was destined.[12] In Chad, a similar study conducted before the country began exporting oil found only 1 percent of nonwage health expenditures on regional health administrations arrived at the health facility level. In Ghana, considered to have one of the better performing public sectors, surveys found leakage rates of 50 percent in education and 80 percent in health.[13]

Even these low efficiency and high leakage rates of social investment assume the money is being allocated toward these efforts in the first place—a lofty assumption for many oil-rich countries. A few years ago the IMF discovered that $32 billion of Angolan government funds were entirely missing from government accounts.[14] Equivalent to 25 percent of Angola's GDP, the $32 billion were spent or transferred from 2007 to 2010 without being documented in the budget. Efforts to improve transparency through initiatives like the Extractive Industries Transparency Initiative (EITI) are well intentioned and undoubtedly valuable, but they are not enough. Nigeria is one of a handful of EITI-compliant nations and yet struggles mightily to spend its oil revenues well. Some standard of transparency is a necessary but not sufficient condition for good revenue management.

Finally, a system of cash transfers is not incompatible with public investments in infrastructure or public services. We are not suggesting that countries move away from all public expenditure toward exclusively private consumption. The government must and should provide certain public goods, such as security, infrastructure, and basic health and education. Distributing part of the revenues, however, can poten-

---

11. Gauthier (2006).
12. Ablo and Reinikka (1998).
13. Gauthier (2006).
14. Human Rights Watch (2011).

tially help oil-rich countries—where the state consumes a disproportionate amount of spending—move toward a better balance between public spending and private consumption.

Moreover, while we typically think of allocating dollars to public versus private consumption as a direct trade-off, the transfer may actually increase both simultaneously, for two reasons. First, deprived of easy oil revenues, the government will be forced to collect taxes to finance itself and its public spending, which potentially brings greater citizen scrutiny and thus could even lead to more public goods delivered per dollar spent. Citizens are more likely to demand real results to investments financed by their own taxes (see objection 8). Whatever efficiency is lost in the transaction costs of distributing the money and taxing it back would likely be more than made up for by efficiency gains, achieved through more closely monitored investments in roads, ports, and schools. In some places, perhaps previously phantom projects would actually get built.

Second, there is reason to believe that public expenditures have diminishing returns to scale. Each dollar allocated toward public spending is less productive than the last, at least in part because of the increased ease of rent-seeking and corruption in countries awash in oil wealth. In light of these diminishing returns to scale, and assuming positive returns to citizen oversight over public investment, transferring rents to citizens can lead to a situation in which a country ends up with more roads, schools, and hospitals *and* more money in citizens' pockets.[15]

3. If We Want to Help People We Should Just Subsidize Food or Other Basic Goods, Create Government Jobs, or Lower Taxes

Most governments already distribute part of their oil revenues to their citizens indirectly. Instead of giving cash transfers to citizens equitably and transparently, however, resource-rich countries often pass on part of the revenues in the form of subsidies and lower taxes. In Saudi Arabia, at 61 cents a gallon, gasoline is cheaper than bottled water, and citizens pay no personal income tax. In Venezuela gasoline is just 6 cents per gallon, and only 9 percent of government revenue comes from direct taxes on citizens and companies.[16]

15. Devarajan and Giugale (2013).
16. Rodriguez, Morales, and Monaldi (2012).

While subsidies are one way of distributing oil rents to citizens, they are inefficient, regressive, highly distortionary, and expensive.[17] Subsidies are extremely costly. Subsidies of oil in Iran amounted to an estimated $100 billion, or 30 percent of GDP, during the high oil prices in 2008.[18] In Nigeria the cost of oil subsidies in 2011 was U.S. $8 billion—more than 25 percent of the federal budget. In addition to gasoline, Saudi Arabia subsidizes drinking water and electricity, at a huge cost to the government: $20 billion for water and $13 billion for electricity.[19] In Egypt alone, subsidies on a range of petroleum products in 2011 accounted for a quarter of the government budget, or around 7 percent of GDP—more than spending on health and education combined.[20]

Besides their steep cost, fuel subsidies are distortionary—they encourage high domestic oil consumption and low fuel efficiency. The distortionary effect of subsidizing oil means that Saudi Arabians (and Nigerians and Venezuelans) are consuming increasingly larger proportions of their oil production, eating away at their export margins. Saudi Arabia currently consumes 3.2 million barrels of oil per day, but at current trends this figure is projected to increase to 8 million barrels per day by 2028, almost equivalent to its entire production.[21]

Finally, fuel subsidies are inefficient and regressive, disproportionately benefiting the wealthy, who own cars and consume the bulk of the subsidized fuels. For instance, Egypt's wealthiest 20 percent have benefited from 34 percent of the value of the energy subsidies, while the poor have benefited from only 13 percent. For gasoline subsidies, the richest quintile received an astonishing 93 percent of the value of the subsidy. Even food subsidies, which should not be regressive, often are: the same report found that the wealthiest 20 percent of Egyptians benefited more from the value of food subsidies than the poorest 20 percent.[22] Subsidies also tend to be largely inefficient and subject to corruption. The cost of

17. The arguments against price subsidies hold true regardless of whether they are financed by natural resource rents. However, to the extent that resource producers are subject to strong political pressures to distribute, subsidies may be particularly prevalent in resource-rich countries.

18. Gelb and Decker (2011).

19. Abeer Allam, "Subsidies Give Saudis an Appetite for Oil," *Financial Times*, May 12, 2011.

20. West (forthcoming).

21. Allam, "Subsidies Give Saudis an Appetite for Oil."

22. World Bank (2005).

delivering one dollar of fuel subsidy to Egypt's poorest 20 percent was estimated to have cost almost $8.[23] Similarly, corruption in Nigeria's fuel subsidy scheme is estimated to have drained U.S. $6.8 billion from government coffers between 2009 and 2011.[24]

Furthermore, once in place, subsidies are extremely difficult, if not impossible, to reverse. Any reduction in subsidies is met with fierce resistance, which in some cases has resulted in political upheaval. The threat of unrest throughout the Arab Spring led to increased subsidies to curb protests. The Tunisian revolt, after all, was in large part spurred by high food prices. In 2010, to soften the blow of the removal of its costly subsidies, Iran turned to cash transfers as a way to build support for a seemingly unbreakable popular defense of subsidies.[25]

Unlike subsidies, universal cash transfers are neither distortionary nor regressive. They help the poor manage food price hikes without distorting the market prices of fuel or energy. And because they represent a significantly higher percentage of income for those in poverty, they are more progressive than subsidies or tax cuts. Cash transfers can be engineered to be less expensive and to smooth out short-term commodity price swings (such as the cost of gasoline). For example, at their 2008 peak of $100 billion, equivalent spending on Iranian subsidies could instead have yielded per capita transfers of $1,400 per year.[26]

Instead of handing out the money, why not simply lower taxes? Doesn't economic theory preach that taxes are distortionary and inefficient, to be avoided except insofar as they are absolutely necessary to raise government revenue or address market failures? Wouldn't the end effect of keeping more money in the pockets of citizens be the same, with much lower transaction costs?

Resource-rich countries do, in fact, tend to have lower taxes. On average, an increase of one percentage point in oil revenues relative to GDP lowers nonoil tax revenues by about 0.2 percent.[27] While low taxes could benefit the business climate and encourage investment to diversify the nonoil economy, resource rents lead to a weaker tax administration that tends to be predatory and regressive. Instead of taxing a broad base

23. World Bank (2005).
24. Mark (2012).
25. Gelb and Decker (2011).
26. Tabatabai (2010).
27. Bornhorst, Gupta, and Thornton (2009).

at low rates, governments tax a narrow taxpaying sector heavily, while large (and powerful) sectors of society escape the tax burden altogether.[28] Tax breaks, moreover, do little to help the poor. A large percentage of the workforce in low-income countries is in the informal sector, which means tax breaks would not affect them—they already pay no taxes.

While lower taxes might keep money in the pockets of citizens, primarily wealthy citizens who have money in their pockets to begin with, their effect on the political economy of governance is largely detrimental. The lack of reliance on taxation destroys the social contract and leads to low accountability and correspondingly poor public service delivery. The standard efficiency arguments against taxation must be carefully weighed against the potential harm (and subsequent inefficiencies) from an unaccountable government.

Yet a third alternative in which oil producers transfer rents to citizens is through expanded levels of public employment for nationals, usually through bloated bureaucracies in inefficient civil administrations. Recent estimates suggest that public sector employment accounts for 80 percent of employment in the oil-rich Gulf States.[29] Oil producers outside the Gulf also tend to have bloated public sectors. The salaries of the 300,000 civil servants in Ecuador alone accounted for 28 percent of the total budget, while the Venezuelan public sector now employs one in six Venezuelan workers.[30]

The prevalence of subsidies and bloated petrobureaucracies is strong evidence of the political pressures for redistribution that come with natural resource wealth. Cash transfers represent just one of the ways in which countries can choose to share the wealth—but a relatively good way. The political reality of oil economies means that the real choice is not between distributing rents or not distributing them but between doing so directly (through universal transfers) or indirectly (through subsidies, low taxes, and public jobs). The former is equitable and generates positive governance externalities; the latter is inequitable, distortive, and clientelist. It is thus against these other indirect distribution systems that cash transfers should be judged.

28. Bornhorst, Gupta, and Thornton (2009).
29. Gelb and Decker (2011).
30. CNN, "With Oil Booms Over, Chávez Vows to Attack Bloated Bureaucracy," May 14, 1999 (http://www.latinamericanstudies.org/venezuela/bureaucracy.htm).

4. We Should Save Our Wealth for the Future, Just as Norway Does

One of the alternatives most often proposed to deal with natural resource revenues is simply to place them in a stabilization fund or a long-term savings fund, and leave it at that. A stabilization fund is designed to smooth public expenditures by protecting government income from short- and medium-term fluctuations in the price of oil.[31] A "future generations" fund saves the funds for later, either to try to provide intergenerational equity or to have funds to use after the (non-renewable) resource has been depleted.

Norway, a wealthy oil-producing country with an aging population, established a sovereign wealth fund to finance its pension system. Russia, on the other hand, facing a different set of constraints, established a stabilization fund primarily to mitigate the fiscal shocks resulting from fluctuations in oil prices. Other countries, like Chile and Ghana, have adopted or are in the process of creating both types of funds. In most cases these funds are held offshore, both for economic reasons (to limit the currency or Dutch disease effects) and for governance reasons (to enable professional fund management and limit political interference).[32]

So why not follow Norway? Because other countries are not Norway. With a GDP per capita of almost $23,000,[33] Norway was a relatively wealthy country when it discovered oil in 1969. Most countries recently discovering oil or likely to discover it in the near future are low-income countries whose development challenges look very different from those faced by Norway in the late sixties. Countries like Liberia and Papua New Guinea have a young, underemployed population, poor human development indicators, and a dearth of serviceable infrastructure. They need an infusion of capital now more than a pension fund to be used for retirement. It makes little sense then to simply copy the Norwegian model under vastly different circumstances.

Creating a Fund Is Not Enough

Certain types of funds, such as stabilization funds that mitigate the fiscal impact of wild swings in oil prices, do make sense in low-income settings.

31. Bell, Heller, and Heuty (2010).
32. Dixon and Monk (2011).
33. Adjusted to 2011 USD, World Bank's World Development Indicators.

Managing oil volatility is a real challenge for oil exporters of all stripes, and a fund could help isolate government budgets from the temptation to overspend when oil prices are high. Many countries, advised by the World Bank and in some cases the Norwegian government itself, have succeeded in setting up stabilization funds. However, setting them up is often the easy part. Once set up, many of these funds fall prey to powerful political pressures to spend the oil money that doom prudent attempts to smooth swings in oil revenues.

In 2001, the World Bank agreed to finance the pipeline linking southern Chadian oil fields to the coast of Cameroon in exchange for Chad's agreement to abide by a strict oil revenue management law drafted in consultation with the bank. The law required Chad to deposit all oil revenues in an escrow account in London managed by an international advisory board and detailed precise rules as to how the Chadian government would allocate the funds, including 10 percent toward a future generations fund. Of the remaining funds, 80 percent had to be spent on certain priority sectors, including health and education, with only 15 percent available for general government operating expenses.[34] The rest of the story is, sadly, fairly predictable. Once the pipeline was built and the oil started flowing, Chadian leaders had no more incentives to abide by the World Bank's rules and proceeded to gradually but blatantly undermine the oil management laws.[35] Some of the first oil revenues were allegedly used to equip the Chadian army with new weapons. Ultimately, after numerous confrontations between Chadian president Déby and the World Bank, Chad prepaid all outstanding World Bank loans relating to the pipeline, and the World Bank formally withdrew from the project.

While the Chadian pipeline fiasco is a prime example of how vulnerable these funds can be to political raids, it is not the only one. In 2004 Nigeria set up an Excess Crude Account in an attempt to prevent harmful volatility, but it too proved inadequate to discipline spending. Not set up as an official sovereign wealth fund, the Excess Crude Account was repeatedly tapped by policymakers, who helped themselves to nearly $17 billion of the $20 billion in the fund.[36] In 2010 Nigeria announced its intention to set up a new and legal sovereign wealth fund to replace

34. Eifert, Gelb, and Tallroth (2002, p. 27).
35. Peg (2009).
36. Dixon and Monk (2011, p. 17).

the Excess Crude Account. However, without anything to safeguard its independence and ensure its integrity, it is unclear why this new sovereign wealth fund would fare any better than its predecessor.

The failed African experiments with sovereign wealth funds demonstrate that by themselves, funds are not enough (see chapter 4). Creating a savings fund does not, in and of itself, change the underlying political economy of the state, nor does it guarantee successful revenue management.[37] Without a politically salient constituency with a vested interest in protecting the savings funds, governments can easily raid them. As a result, these funds are at best ineffective and at worst counterproductive: they could effectively transfer funds from responsible governments (which save them) to irresponsible ones (which raid them).

Not all sovereign wealth funds are doomed to fail. Countries with a sufficiently strong political constituency invested in the well-being of the fund have had successful sovereign wealth funds. In Botswana, politically influential cattle ranchers had a strong interest in keeping the exchange rate stable by adopting prudent macroeconomic stabilization policies, and political elites had little need for patronage spending owing to the overwhelming dominance of the ruling party.[38] When diamond rents came on stream in the 1970s, powerful interests complied with existing institutions to avoid rocking the boat and disrupting the stream of wealth.[39] This politically salient cattle-ranching constituency provided precisely the type of influential watchdog that contributed to the success of the Pula Fund.

By giving citizens a direct stake in the integrity of a sovereign wealth fund, a universal cash transfer system can create a politically salient constituency where no such constituency exists. The most telling evidence of this comes from Alaska. The success of Alaska's Permanent Fund, which now stands at $43 billion, owes much to the protection of the constituency built around the annual dividend. Tellingly, while Alaska is famous for wasting federal funds on "bridges to nowhere," the billions of dollars in the principal fund are inviolable. Touching them is seen as an attack on the dividend itself, and politicians steer clear of it for fear of political backlash.

37. Dixon and Monk (2011).
38. Moss and Young (2009).
39. Acemoglu, Johnson, and Robinson (2002).

Most important, these options are not mutually exclusive. Regardless of their final destination, oil producers can and should employ a stabilization fund to promote transparency, mitigate volatility, and ring-fence oil revenues in any spending scenario. The experiences of Nigeria and Chad, however, make it clear that success with sovereign wealth funds alone is less than assured.

5. Giving People Cash Will Only Stoke Inflation and Wipe Out Any Welfare Gains

Injecting millions of dollars into a cash-strapped economy seems like the perfect recipe for an inflationary disaster. Money going into the pockets of every citizen will lead to a surge in demand for consumer goods. If the local economy is unable to match the demand with increased supply (perhaps because of trade barriers or insufficient local production capacity), it could result in inflationary pressure that could dull or even cancel out the benefits of the cash transfer.

While the risk of inflation is real and should not be underestimated, inflation is not inevitable. Inflationary pressures can be mitigated through careful monetary policy, which will be necessary in any case because of the inflow of foreign capital. The government can also take steps to alleviate supply-side constraints, such as reducing import barriers.

Experience with cash transfer programs shows that the impact of inflation can be mitigated through program design. For instance, capping the transfer at a modest level and gradually increasing the size of the payments could allow production capacity to build up over time. The Bolivian pension program financed by natural gas receipts paid pensioners on their birthday, which distributed the payments over time and resulted in the program having a negligible impact on inflation.[40]

Moreover, the relative inflationary risk of cash transfers depends strongly on the counterfactual. Saving revenue in a sovereign wealth fund would have no inflationary impact as long as the funds were held offshore. However, capital-starved economies with underemployed populations are not realistically going to save all the rents for the future—

40. This strategy might not be desirable or even possible in universal cash transfers, but it does suggest that program design can help mitigate inflationary pressures. See Laserna (forthcoming).

nor should they. Thus, cash transfers should be judged against the true counterfactual of increased government expenditure.

There is no compelling reason to believe that private individual spending will be more inflationary than public sector spending. Public spending on infrastructure and civil service wages will likely generate the same kind of demand-side pressures. Unless public spending goes toward investments that alleviate supply-side constraints, inflation will remain a concern. Of course, if public spending ends up in corrupt government officials' foreign bank accounts instead of in civil servants' wages, it will have no impact on inflation at all. Yet it is hard to argue that would be a better outcome.

The better question is how to ensure that the government undertakes the kinds of investments that will loosen production constraints. In a system of public expenditures that is largely unaccountable, there may be more pressure for patronage spending than for broad infrastructure projects as governments use rents to maintain the political support of key allies. In a system of cash transfers there is both a demand for these types of investments (from increased private sector activity) and interest from the government in promoting the broader economic well-being, as government revenues are now tied to tax receipts that will rise alongside economic productivity (discussed in chapter 5).

If inflation is the primary concern, however, the trade-off is not between public and private consumption but rather between spending and saving.

6. Regular Dividends Will Create Laziness and Discourage Work

It is tempting to believe that giving people a regular cash transfer will either create an unsustainable dependency on government handouts or harm the labor market. The evidence, however, tells a different story.

To start, there is no conclusive evidence that modest cash transfers reduce labor market participation overall.[41] Standard economic theory suggests that an increase in income would lead to a decline in the supply of labor, potentially harming long-term growth. Yet a number of studies suggest empirically that this effect is mitigated for extremely poor households, and is outweighed by positive effects.[42]

41. DFID-UK (2011).
42. Barrientos and Scott (2008).

Insofar as cash transfers have been shown to decrease labor supply, the decrease tends to be in the labor supply of children and the elderly. With a steady income from pensions, labor force participation among the elderly has been shown to decrease considerably.[43] Several studies have also found that a regular cash income enables parents to send their children to school instead of work, and has reduced child labor by as much as 17 percent in Ecuador and 26 percent in Brazil's Bahia state.[44] However, this decrease (positive in and of itself) is complemented by other positive effects, so that cash transfers may even increase labor supply.

When children are in school and grandparents are available to provide childcare, parents can work longer hours or migrate farther in search of more productive work. In South Africa, households that received the old-age pension had 11–12 percent higher labor participation rates and 8–15 percent higher employment rates than those who did not receive a pension. In Brazil, the labor participation was 2.6 percentage points higher for those in the Bolsa Família program than for those not in the program, a difference that was even greater for women.[45] Cash transfers enable less productive members of households to remain at home, thereby freeing up more productive members to migrate to find better economic opportunities. Increased household spending on health and nutrition has also been shown to increase the productivity of workers and decrease the productivity lost to illness.[46]

Moreover, the risk of labor disincentives can be mitigated through smart program design. The effects of winning the lottery versus earning an extra $10 a month on someone's willingness to work are drastically different. The size of the transfers could be capped at a ratio of average national income—for instance, 10 percent of average per capita income: enough to boost the income of the poorest but not large enough to replace labor income. Of note, a universal cash transfer without means testing ensures that there are no perverse incentives that could discourage labor. Eligibility conditions tied to income represent effectively high marginal tax rates, which create perverse incentives to stay eligible.

43. Barrientos and Scott (2008, p. 3).
44. Edmonds (2006); Rawlings and Rubio (2003).
45. DFID-UK (2011).
46. DFID-UK (2011).

7. People Will Just Waste Cash on Consumption

Ordinary people, it is sometimes argued, will waste the resources on frivolous consumption. Yet there are definitional, moral, and empirical reasons why this objection does not hold up to scrutiny.

Definitional: You say consumption, I say investment. What is often considered by economists to be "consumption" (as opposed to "investment") may be exactly the kind of welfare-enhancing outcomes hoped for by policymakers. Enhanced consumption for the majority of those living near or below the poverty line means improved nutrition and living standards. Thus, for the poor, greater spending on food, housing, and other day-to-day expenses is not really consumption but rather investment in future human capital.

Moral: It's about freedom to choose. There are principled reasons to believe that people, no matter how poor or rural or uneducated, know what is in their own best interests better than bureaucrats in faraway capitals. Development, after all, is in essence about freeing people from the constraints of poverty, not dictating how they should lead their lives.[47] By providing a regular, assured income, Oil-to-Cash can do precisely that—allow the poorest the freedom to make the decisions that maximize their own welfare.

Empirical: Evidence proves poor people use money wisely. Studies suggest that cash transfers tend to lead to increased spending on health, nutrition, sanitation, and education.[48] There is strong evidence of significant positive relationships between pension receipt and improved health outcomes for both children and adults living in the households of pensioners.[49] Similarly positive results are recorded for education outcomes, such as enrollment and attendance, for some members of households receiving cash transfers.[50] This improved human capital should raise labor productivity in the present and future, although the long-term impacts are hard to measure empirically because of the relative novelty of transfers.

And while the bulk of the amount transferred is generally spent on improved consumption, there is some evidence that a small but important

---

47. Sen (1999).
48. Case (2001); Yanez-Pagans (2008).
49. Case (2001); Duflo (2003).
50. Edmonds (2006); de Carvalho Filho (2008); Akee and others (2008); Baird, McIntosh, and Özler (2011).

portion of the cash transfer is invested in productive activities or used to cover the cost of job-seeking. A regular assured income serves as insurance that allows poor people to make risky investments with potential high returns that they otherwise could not afford for fear of falling below subsistence level (such as planting high-yield instead of drought-resistant crops).[51] For every peso transferred to families through Mexico's Oportunidades, recipients spent 88 cents on consumer goods and invested the rest. And while that might not sound like much, investments were impressively lucrative, with an average rate of return of almost 18 percent, which raised their consumption beyond the period of the transfer itself.[52] Similar experiences in Ethiopia, Zambia, and Paraguay provide growing evidence of cash transfers fostering increased investment and risk-taking.

8. Oil-to-Cash Won't Create Any Incentives to Hold the Government to Account

Is it realistic to expect that government accountability will magically materialize simply because citizens pay taxes? Why would an ordinary citizen suddenly start paying attention to government budgets and spending priorities just because the money comes in theory from her pockets and not from oil rents?

Of course, not every citizen will devote her life to monitoring government spending just because she pays taxes—nor should she. This is certainly not the case in even the most developed countries with broad-based tax systems. However, compared to the counterfactual for most oil exporters, a cash transfer system tied to a broad taxation scheme does fundamentally alter citizens' incentives and capacity to hold the government accountable.

Taxation has three effects on citizens' demand for accountability: it increases incentives to monitor by raising the perceived cost of waste; it decreases the cost of monitoring by revealing information; and it builds the capacity to hold the government accountable by giving citizens (through their representatives) the power of the purse.

It raises the stakes. Distributing oil funds directly to citizens provides them with a direct incentive to actively participate in monitoring the revenue flow. It is one thing for citizens to be apathetic about yet another

51. DFID-UK (2011, p. 35).
52. Gertler, Martinez, and Rubio-Codina (2006).

white elephant project or an unkempt road when the funds wasted were never within their reach. It is quite another when misappropriated funds come from taxes, or when squandered oil revenues result in a measurable decrease in cash payments. And while certain civil society groups may be monitoring the government without such incentives anyway, there is an important difference between a few watchdog organizations and the entire citizenry having a personal stake in good revenue management.

It reveals the government's cards. To monitor the government effectively, citizens need information: the amount of money flowing into government coffers, the amount flowing out, and how much money arrives at its intended destination. All this information is costly to obtain, particularly in countries with opaque public expenditure systems. Distributing a share of resource revenues and taxing part of it back reveals important information about government revenues and should lead to greater citizen monitoring of government expenditure. The more information citizens have, the more effective the monitoring will be, and thus the more likely they will find it worthwhile to monitor. Distribution and taxation, in other words, decrease the cost of monitoring for citizens.[53] As part of the early public education campaign, the government could use billboards or radio programs (or produce cards like that shown in figure 4-1) to explain exactly how the dividend was calculated, where the money came from, and what portion is being taxed.

It equips citizens with a bargaining tool. Having incentives to monitor the government is not, unfortunately, enough. Citizens also need the capacity to influence the government. Old European monarchies did not relinquish power and dole out greater rights out of benevolence. Greater rights and accountability were the steep price they had to pay for the funds they needed to finance costly wars.[54] No rights, no funds. In resource-rich countries where the government has access to oil rents, citizens lack this bargaining chip. Even if citizens are able to monitor government spending and keep tabs on how much ends up in foreign bank accounts instead of schools, they often find themselves powerless to change it. Governments that do not depend on citizens for funding have little need to pay attention to their demands.

In this way taxation represents a major shift in the balance of power from the government to citizens, who through their representatives in

53. For the complete model and assumptions, see Devarajan and others (2011).
54. Tilly (1975); Bräutigam, Fjeldstat, and Moore (2008).

parliament can now withhold funds unless the government delivers on its end of the bargain. No schools and no roads means no taxes. Taxation is the only way of ensuring that governments act on behalf of the governed, and while it works imperfectly even in the most developed countries, it is better than the alternative.

Recent evidence suggests that this kind of revenue bargaining is not limited to the rise of Western representative systems centuries ago.[55] A fascinating modern-day insight into how bargaining can lead to more responsive governance comes from Somaliland, a region that by virtue of its lack of international recognition as an independent state is barred from foreign development assistance and thus relies solely on local taxes for all government revenue. Deprived of alternatives, the government of Somaliland was forced to bargain with local business leaders, providing a set of representative institutions with checks and balances in return for the revenues needed to finance the government. In 1999, taxpayers provided 95 percent of the government's resources. This dependence on taxes imposes limits on the executive that neighboring leaders have been able to completely bypass.[56]

While this type of explicit bargaining may depend on the presence of small cohesive groups, it is not exclusive to Somaliland. Studies have found evidence of such bargains by migrant herders in Senegal, elite taxpayers in Latin America, and sugar exporters in Mauritius.[57] Even when no such cohesive groups are found, however, there is growing empirical evidence that taxation may lead to more demands for accountability and thus improved public service delivery. Timmons, for instance, shows that regressive taxation is associated with higher public goods provision to the poorest, while progressive taxation is associated with stronger property rights for wealthy taxpayers; in other words, the government caters to the poor when they pay a bigger share of the tax burden, and vice versa.[58] Meanwhile, new cross-country, subnational, and experimental studies are starting to provide evidence of a link between taxation and accountability that is less outdated than pointing back to the Magna Carta and American cries for independence (see box 5-1).

55. Moore (2008, p. 26).
56. Eubank (2012).
57. Juul (2006); Mahon (2004); Bräutigam (2008).
58. Timmons (2005).

A reliance on taxation for government revenue also aligns the incentives of the government with the well-being of the economy. Whereas governments that survive on natural-resource rents are indifferent to the fate of the nonoil economy, once revenues start to rise and fall with the fate of the broader economy, it is in the self-interest of governments to foster economic development. More firms, more workers, and more foreign investors paying taxes all mean more money in government coffers. There is evidence that strong pressure to put an end to a conflict in Somaliland between the government and the Habar Yonis clan resulted from insistent taxpayers whose businesses depended on peace and stability.[59] Taxation might not be a quick fix for all the woes of resource-rich nations, but it does help align incentives between governments and citizens toward broader economic well-being.

There is a growing consensus that broad-based taxation is an essential part of building sustainable and accountable institutions in developing countries.[60] The great challenge for the resource-rich is trying to create this broad tax base precisely when the government feels it can do without one.

9. It Is Impossible to Implement Oil-to-Cash Where There Is No National Identification System and Few People Have Bank Accounts

It may seem contradictory to argue that a government incapable of wisely using oil rents to build roads and schools will be able to transfer large amounts of money to its entire citizenry. Concerns of corruption and leakage in the management of public finances of oil producers might make many nervous about entrusting those same governments with distributing large amounts of cash. However, cash transfers currently reach millions of people in low-income countries, a good indication that they are not unfeasible. Moreover, with the advent of and greater access to new biometric and financial technologies, cash transfer systems are becoming increasingly low-cost, efficient, and secure from fraud. As Alan Gelb and Caroline Decker have concluded, these new

59. Eubank (2012).
60. Moore (2007); McGuirk (2010); Bräutigam, Fjeldstat, and Moore (2008); Ross (2012).

technologies mean that "the barriers to transfers are no longer technical, but political."[61]

It's already being done. Transferring funds to the entire population of a poor country may seem daunting, yet it is already being done. Developing and emerging market governments in more than sixty countries made regular payments to some 170 million people as of 2009.[62] This included forty-nine social protection programs (unconditional, conditional, or workfare payments), as well as payments of wages or pensions from the government to low-income citizens, which often dwarf social protection programs in size (see table 2-1). The number of people covered by transfers has undoubtedly grown since then, and will continue to do so as countries like Iran and India keep rolling out sizable transfer programs.

Any payment system should accomplish two functions: verification of identity and transfer of funds. In recent years two technologies, biometric identification and mobile banking, have made such cash payments both feasible and potentially low-cost.

Identification: Biometrics. One of the main concerns of passing out cash to a large population is minimizing fraud and corruption. Unique identifiers, particularly new biometric identifiers, can play an important role in preventing leakage in the form of payments to ghost citizens or noncitizens or double payments. Biometric identification methods (such as fingerprinting or iris scanning) have fortunately become widespread, and costs are declining. More than a billion people in developing countries have already had their biometric data recorded.[63]

Biometric identifiers have been used to support cash transfer programs in more than eleven countries, successfully reducing fraudulent registrations (and therefore leakage) wherever implemented. Biometric audits in Nigeria cut the number of federal pensions by almost 40 percent, with impressive savings also reported in Botswana and the Indian state of Andhra Pradesh.[64]

Delivery: Electronic payments and branchless banking. Paying with physical cash, which has been the norm in many places, comes with great costs and risks. Today, even in the poorest countries, electronic

61. Gelb and Decker (2011).
62. Pickens, Porteous, and Rotman (2009).
63. Gelb and Clark (2013).
64. Gelb and Clark (2013).

payment and transfer systems are gaining popularity. Electronic delivery can take the form of direct deposit into bank accounts, providing debit cards, or transferring funds through basic accounts linked to mobile banking. Already, about half of social transfer programs launched over the past decade feature some type of electronic payment, with two important benefits: lower transaction costs and transparent, auditable payment trails.[65]

Electronic payments can be deposited straight into existing bank accounts, but new branchless banking technology opens the door for wider coverage of areas underserved by the traditional financial sector. Even where the banking system may not provide universal coverage, the mobile prepaid card vendor network usually does. With new mobile financial services, governments can deposit money directly into citizens' mobile cellphone accounts.

Whatever form it takes, electronic delivery can significantly reduce the administrative costs of a transfer. When Brazil's Bolsa Família switched to electronic benefit cards, administrative costs dropped nearly sevenfold, from 14.7 percent of the grant value to 2.6 percent. In South Africa, the cost of transfers dropped by 62 percent after the program switched to depositing in bank accounts offered by the private sector.[66]

Another crucial benefit of using electronic payments is that such systems allow auditors to trace funds from the issuer to the final recipient, a major safeguard against corruption. While it is true that no system can be watertight against fraud, it is also worth remembering the counterfactual of other options. In the case of Ghana, the funds lost though public sector spending were 50–80 percent. By comparison, a hypothetical 1 million fraudulent recipients (such as ghost recipients or noncitizens illegally claiming a transfer) would be the equivalent of about a 4 percent leakage.

10. Maybe Oil-to-Cash Is a Good Idea, but No Politician Will Ever Do It

Instituting an Oil-to-Cash program will certainly require political foresight and a level of confidence that may be unusual. However, it is not unfathomable. A number of countries are already implementing

65. Pickens, Porteous, and Rotman (2009).
66. Pickens, Porteous, and Rotman (2009).

resource-backed cash transfers, so clearly, politicians in Alaska, Mongolia, Bolivia, and elsewhere saw some political calculation that made this attractive.

The question is, what could make Oil-to-Cash politically palatable elsewhere? What might convince politicians to try it? Theoretically, at least, one could think of a number of characteristics that would facilitate the political implementation of an Oil-to-Cash scheme.[67] Leaders of resource-rich countries often use rents strategically to consolidate their hold on power and are therefore most likely to adopt a universal cash transfer scheme when they value the support of a broad electorate that would benefit from the policy. Thus, a fairly open democracy, a post-conflict period in which leaders are trying to cement national unity, or a strong leader seeking to solidify his or her personal popularity would all potentially find it in their interest to adopt such a scheme.[68] In addition, countries that have not yet received oil income or that face a constitutional moment (such as the post–Arab Spring countries) may be good candidates since the barriers from entrenched interests are presumably lower.

This is roughly what has happened in practice. Cash transfers funded by oil revenues targeted at veterans and internally displaced persons in Timor-Leste were aimed at creating postconflict stability by co-opting potential sources of renewed violence into the system. Other oil-rich, conflict-prone countries, such as Iraq and Colombia, might be tempted to follow suit.[69] The fact that Timor-Leste became an oil producer only in 2005 meant that it had relative freedom to use the oil revenues without upsetting entrenched interests. Countries recently discovering oil and natural gas reserves, such as Ghana, Uganda, and Liberia, might have an advantage establishing this kind of scheme over long-time producers.

Occasionally, a visionary politician like former Alaska governor Jay Hammond will establish an oil dividend looking to tie his own hands and those of his successors, to protect the state from careless spending.[70] However, no such uncommon self-restraint or farsighted vision is nec-

67. For a more detailed discussion of these issues, see Gillies (2010).
68. Gillies (2010, p. 1).
69. There is growing support among certain political circles in Iraq for this kind of proposal; see West (2011).
70. Governor Jay Hammond was supported in his vision by an Alaskan populace that feared a continuation of the reckless spending that befell the initial oil windfall

essary. Distributing oil revenues may in some cases be a savvy strategy to garner political support.

Politicians may simply recognize that promoting a proposal to put cash in the hands of their constituents could become quickly and deeply popular. Bolivia's cash transfers funded from resource revenues were introduced by President Sánchez de Lozada allegedly to build support for the 1997 election. While opposition politicians initially denounced it, once it gained popularity with voters, resistance became politically dangerous, and both sides embraced the proposal.[71] Similarly, the Mongolian Child Money Program, funded through mineral revenues, arose out of competition between political parties vying for support during the 2004 general elections.[72] A large rise in mineral revenues in the early 2000s prompted opposition politicians to argue that citizens had not benefited enough from the country's mineral wealth. This led to a bidding war between the governing party and the opposition over various cash transfer programs and the ultimate adoption of the Child Money Program under a coalition government.[73] More recently, oil-funded cash transfers have been adopted by governments desperate to find a politically palatable way to roll back subsidies. India and Iran have both resorted to cash transfers to soften the removal of costly fuel subsidies.[74]

While none of these programs is a perfect model of the universal distribution of revenues proposed here,[75] they are all variations of resource-rent distribution and involve comparable political calculations. Their precedence demonstrates that, though politically challenging to implement, distribution carries political benefits that render it feasible.

Once the program is in place, it becomes politically costly to eliminate. Attempts to stop the Bolivian pension system by a successor president were met with stiff resistance and led to the reelection of Bonosol's architect Sánchez de Lozada on a promise to reinstate and strengthen it. Evo Morales, who viewed his predecessor as his nemesis, not only kept

---

and was concerned with an equitable distribution of the benefits for all citizens (see Goldsmith [2012]).

71. For a full account of the Bolivia story, see Laserna (forthcoming).

72. Hodges and others (2007).

73. Hodges and others (2007).

74. Gelb and Decker (2011).

75. Neither the Bolivia nor the Timor-Leste program is universal, while the Mongolia Child Money Program has expanded to attain quasi-universality but remains a

the program, but expanded it.[76] Similarly, the oil dividend in Alaska has rendered the Alaska Permanent Fund invulnerable to the myopia of political spending. Even though the Alaskan dividend is not constitutionally guaranteed, its enormous popularity makes legislators so wary of decreasing the payments that they have gone so far as to make contributions to the fund beyond the mandated amount in order to increase the dividend.[77] It may also be the case that once one country establishes a dividend system, other countries will feel pressure to follow suit. Mexico's conditional cash transfer experience raised expectations in Brazil, and then in Argentina and Chile, and so on.

Oil-to-cash is, of course, a deeply political choice, requiring a political leader to seize on the idea and push through objections and special interests. In countries where no prominent politician champions the idea, adoption is highly unlikely. In light of the growing belief that natural resources belong to all citizens, however, maintaining the status quo in which rents accrue to a small elite will perhaps become increasingly indefensible. Once several more countries take the Oil-to-Cash path, it could even become a new norm.

---

conditional transfer. India's and Iran's programs are universal but are not aimed at broad revenue management. Alaska comes closest, as it is a universal program, but since Alaska eliminated the personal income tax in a compromise to pass the Permanent Fund bill, it lacks the crucial taxation component. Permanent Fund architect and former governor Jay Hammond later believed that eliminating taxes was a huge mistake because, in his words, it effectively "cut the cord that attaches the public's purse to the fingers of the politicians" (Hammond [2012]).

76. Laserna (forthcoming).
77. Goldsmith (2012, p.13).

7

Where Might Oil-to-Cash Happen?

This book has articulated the rationale for providing citizens with a direct cash stake in their country's natural resource wealth. We've made the case that Oil-to-Cash benefits both citizens and governments by transferring cash into the hands of the people while rebuilding the social contract that a flow of oil or mineral revenues into the government coffers typically weakens or destroys. We have anticipated and attempted to answer a range of objections. One key question remains: which countries are best positioned to actually try Oil-to-Cash? The history of development is loaded with examples of good ideas on paper that fail when confronted with complex and messy realities. We are well aware that Oil-to-Cash is a proposal that will become substantially messier when it is tried in the real world. We are also cognizant that the idea doesn't apply everywhere, and, where it is attempted, it will have to be significantly adapted to local political and economic conditions. Nevertheless, in this chapter we attempt to identify the most promising candidate countries by teasing out some of the factors that might make an Oil-to-Cash scheme economically desirable and politically feasible.

Are Economic Conditions Right for Rolling Out Oil-to-Cash?

Does Oil-to-Cash make economic sense for all oil and gas producers? No. Some oil and mineral exporters, such as Norway, Botswana, and

Chile, appear able to manage the pressures of windfall gains and to funnel their resource rents into government budgets that are subject to relatively tight systems of accountability and oversight. In countries with strong traditions of effective institutions and largely accountable governments, the transaction costs of distributing and taxing back oil and mineral revenues may outweigh the governance benefits. This is not to say that these countries might not benefit from creating citizen shareholders but that a radical departure from the typical spending approach may not be necessary.

But for most oil and mineral exporters, this is not the case. In many countries there is little confidence that money poured into the black box of the government budget will be used productively. It is these countries, which would otherwise most likely "waste" their oil and mineral revenues, that would benefit the most from an Oil-to-Cash system.

How can these ideal candidates be identified? We suggest that an Oil-to-Cash approach makes economic sense in any given country where four factors are present: abundant natural resources coupled with high levels of economic dependence on these resources, low capacity to implement and monitor public investments or prevent corruption, an otherwise dysfunctional business environment, and an existing system for distributing oil and mineral revenues that is highly distortive or inefficient.[1]

Resource Abundance Coupled with Resource Dependence

Countries with abundant oil resources per capita and in which oil makes up a large percentage of the economy are the best Oil-to-Cash candidates. Oil abundance and oil dependence are distinct indicators. Abundance (having a lot of oil per capita) is a measure of the potential size of an Oil-to-Cash transfer.[2] Countries with plentiful oil resources will be able to transfer meaningful dividends to citizens and to fund (through withheld or other taxes) government expenditures. For instance, distributing 10 percent of oil revenues to all citizens in Uganda, a country

1. This section draws heavily on Arezki, Dupuy, and Gelb (2012).

2. The stock of available natural resources is as important as the flow in determining the feasibility and size of a potential Oil-to-Cash program. However, current reserves are not necessarily an accurate indication of natural wealth. New research suggests that improved rates of discovery, spurred by technological change and market conditions, mean that countries can continue to generate resource rents for longer than indicated by current reserve estimates. See Gelb, Kaiser, and Viñuela (2012).

with modest oil windfalls, would yield an annual dividend of $2 per person, whereas distributing the same percentage in Equatorial Guinea would yield an annual dividend of $642 per person.[3]

On the other hand, oil-dependent countries (those in which oil makes up a large percentage of national income or fiscal revenues) are likely to reap the most benefit from an Oil-to-Cash system, as resource dependence is highly correlated with poor resource governance (see chapter 3). Larger commodity windfalls are associated with greater rent-seeking behavior, which weakens a country's capacity to invest.[4] Countries with higher dependence on oil also tend to be those in which the public sector makes up a disproportionate part of the economy, and as a result, public investment is likely to have low marginal returns. Oil dependence thus makes oil dividends more desirable, while oil abundance makes them more feasible (see table 7-1).

Weak Public Administrative Capacity

To invest oil revenues successfully, governments need to identify, implement, and monitor investments that support the development of the nonresource private sector.[5] This requires administrative capacity. It also involves achieving a degree of control over corruption, so that enough money actually reaches the intended destination. Administrative capacity and control of corruption, however, tend to be particularly weak in most resource-rich states.[6] Some oil exporters may very well strengthen their investment capacity in the medium term. Yet such an improvement is unlikely to happen overnight, if it happens at all: in a context awash with oil money, incentives frequently run in the opposite direction. Large commodity windfalls often induce lower, not higher, levels of public investment as officials seek to appropriate

3. Devarajan and Giugale (2013).
4. A study of thirty oil-exporting countries between 1992 and 2005 found that large oil windfalls were correlated with a significant increase in corruption, which raised the cost of public investment and reduced its quality (Arezki and Brückner [2011]).
5. Arezki, Dupuy, and Gelb (2012).
6. The IMF's Public Investment Management Index, which measures countries' public investment efficiency across four categories (project appraisal, selection, implementation, and evaluation), finds that oil exporters and low-income countries have weaker public investment management, but with significant cross-country variation (Dabla-Norris and others [2011]).

TABLE 7-1. Top Oil Producers

Country	Annual oil production per capita (in barrels, 2009–13 average)	R/P ratio[a] (2013)	Country	Annual oil production per capita (in barrels, 2009–13 average)	R/P ratio[a] (2013)
Qatar	343.3	34.4	United States	9.7	12.1
Kuwait	332.3	89	Mexico	9.0	10.6
Equatorial Guinea	165.4	15	Malaysia	8.6	15.3
Norway	151.7	12.9	Australia	8.1	26.1
Brunei	143.8	22.3	Colombia	6.7	6.5
Saudi Arabia	141.8	63.2	United Kingdom	6.7	9.6
United Arab Emirates	133.4	73.5	Argentina	6.2	9.8
Oman	105.3	16	Nigeria	5.3	43.8
Libya	75.5	100+	Syria	4.5	100+
Gabon	56.5	23.1	Brazil	3.9	20.2
Kazakhstan	38.2	46	Yemen	3.7	51.2
Canada	37.6	100+	Chad	3.3	43.5
Azerbaijan	37.5	21.9	Egypt	3.3	15
Trinidad and Tobago	37.2	19.2	Sudan	3.0	33.7
Venezuela	34.5	100+	Tunisia	2.5	18.7
Angola	32.5	19.3	Thailand	2.3	2.5
Iraq	32.1	100+	South Sudan	2.1	96.9
Russian Federation	26.8	23.6	Romania	1.6	19
Republic of the Congo			Indonesia	1.4	11.6
(Brazzaville)	24.8	15.6	Vietnam	1.4	34.5
Iran	19.6	100+	Peru	1.3	37.5
Algeria	15.9	21.2	China	1.1	11.9
Turkmenistan	15.7	7.1	Uzbekistan	1.0	25.9
Denmark	14.7	10.3	Italy	0.7	32.7
Ecuador	12.0	42.6			

Source: Authors' calculations from British Petroleum Statistical Review of World Energy 2014 and the World Bank's World Development Index data.

a. The reserves-to-production (R/P) ratio is the number of years that the producer could keep producing oil at current rates out of proven reserves.

resources.[7] In the meantime, poor public investment capacity (as measured by the IMF's Public Investment Management Index, for instance) and high levels of corruption (scoring poorly on the World Bank's governance metrics, for example) provide possible rough criteria to identify countries that would most benefit from distributing oil revenues to citizens rather than investing them directly (see figures 7-1, 7-2, and 7-3).

7. Arezki, Dupuy, and Gelb (2012).

FIGURE 7-1. **Country Scores on IMF Public Investment Management Index[a]**

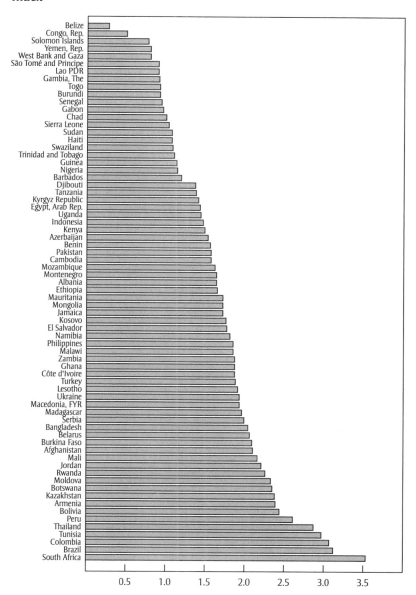

Source: Dabla-Norris and others (2011).

a. The IMF Public Investment Management Index is a composite index denoting the efficiency of the public investment management process, with scores ranging from 0 (worst) to 4 (best). Seventeen individual indicators of the quality and efficiency of the investment process are measured across four consecutive stages: project appraisal, selection, implementation, and evaluation. For a detailed methodology, see Dabla-Norris and others (2011).

FIGURE 7-2. **Corruption and Natural Resource Dependence**

WGI Control of Corruption Index (2011, percentile rank)

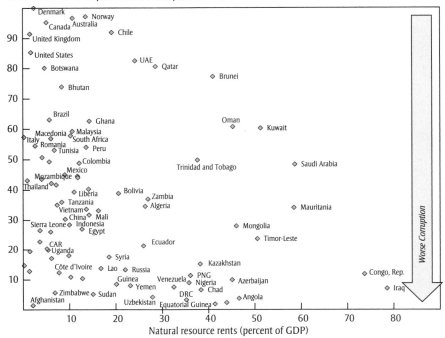

Sources: World Bank's World Governance Indicators (WGI), Control of Corruption Index (http://info.worldbank.org/governance/wgi/index.aspx#home). Natural resource rents from World Bank, World Development Indicators. Doing Business from World Bank Group's Doing Business (http://www.doingbusiness.org).

Note: The Control of Corruption Index measures the extent to which public power is exercised for private gain, including both petty and grand corruption. The index compiles data from more than twenty sources on the prevalence and depth of corruption, as well as on government efforts to combat it. A higher percentile rank indicates lower levels of corruption across the indicators.

Dysfunctional Business Climate

An unfavorable business climate undermines the potential for public capital to generate private investment by diminishing the extent to which private actors respond to opportunities created by public infrastructure.[8] Investing oil revenues in a new port or road will attract manufacturers who need to transport and ship goods abroad. Few businesses will take advantage of the new infrastructure, however, if red tape and bureaucracy make acquiring permits prohibitively costly, or if weak

8. Arezki, Dupuy, and Gelb (2012).

FIGURE 7-3. Corruption and Resource Abundance

WGI Control of Corruption Index (2011, percentile rank)

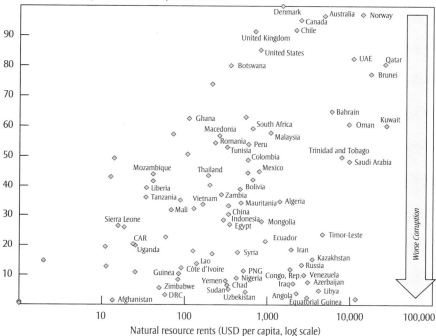

Sources: See figure 7-2.

Notes: See note in figure 7-2. Natural resource rents per capita is a measure of the country's natural resource wealth. It is calculated by the World Bank as the sum of oil rents, natural gas rents, coal rents, mineral rents, and forest rents. Each of those represents the value of the production of these natural resources minus the total cost of production. Of note, this is not equivalent to fiscal revenues from hydrocarbons to the government, which will be lower, as governments only capture a fraction of the total rents.

rule of law means companies cannot enforce contracts, or if regulations are deliberately designed to extract resource rents and squelch entrepreneurship. In other words, poor business climates reduce the returns on public investment, and thus increase the optimal level of cash transfers.[9] Figures 7-5 and 7-6 rank countries along the World Bank's Doing Business rankings and a measure of resource dependence/abundance. Countries that have poor business climates and high levels of dependence/abundance (those toward the bottom right corner) are good candidates for Oil-to-Cash.

9. Arezki, Dupuy, and Gelb (2012) proxy the business climate with a lower total factor productivity in the nonresource sector.

BOX 7-1. Measuring Resource Management and Transparency

The Revenue Watch Institute's 2013 Resource Governance Index measures the quality of governance in the oil, gas, and mining sectors in fifty-eight countries, which are ranked on four governance components. The index finds that only eleven of the fifty-eight top resource exporters have satisfactory standards of accountability and transparency (see figure 7-4). "Satisfactory" denotes a score above 70 on the composite score. The four subcomponents are Institutional and Legal Setting, Reporting Practices, Safeguards and Quality Controls, and Enabling Environment. (For a detailed methodology, see Revenue Watch [2013]). Although it focuses on upstream transparency and governance—that is, on whether countries, for example, publish contracts, join the Extractive Industries Transparency Initiative, or provide citizens with access to information on the amount and sources of resource revenues—rather than on the expenditure side, the Resource Governance Index provides an additional measure of revenue management capacity. Countries with larger "resource governance deficits" according to the Resource Governance Index should, all other things being equal, be those that could most benefit from oil dividends and the demand for transparency these dividends would be expected to generate.

Highly Distortive or Inefficient Resource Distribution

Many resource-rich countries do distribute some resource revenues to citizens, but they do so indirectly. Typically, some export revenues are spent on subsidies for basic goods, often fuel. Subsidies of this kind are, despite popular expectations, almost everywhere deeply regressive, as those who benefit the most are the upper and middle classes (see chapter 3).

Subsidies can also become extremely expensive (see figure 7-7 and table 7-2). In Egypt, subsidies on a range of petroleum products recently accounted for more than a quarter of the government budget, or around 6.7 percent of GDP—more than spending on health and education combined.[10] Nigeria faced similar budget-gobbling dynamics in 2011, with a subsidy costing a whopping 4.7 percent of GDP, disproportionately benefiting the wealthy and encouraging widespread smuggling and corruption.[11]

Subsidies, however, can offer an opportunity to introduce the concept of a national cash transfer. Iran, for instance, explicitly decided to replace subsidies for basic goods with cheaper and more efficient cash

---

10. West (forthcoming).
11. IMF (2013).

FIGURE 7-4. **Revenue Watch Institute's Resource Governance Index (2013), by Country**[a]

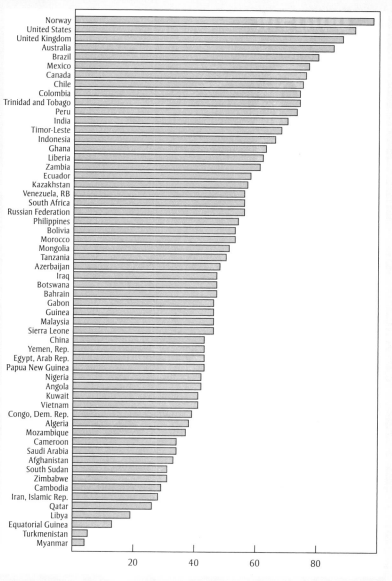

Sources: See figure 7-2.
a. Lower aggregate scores represent worse natural resource governance.

FIGURE 7-5.   Business Climate and Resource Dependence

Doing Business ranking (out of 185 countries)

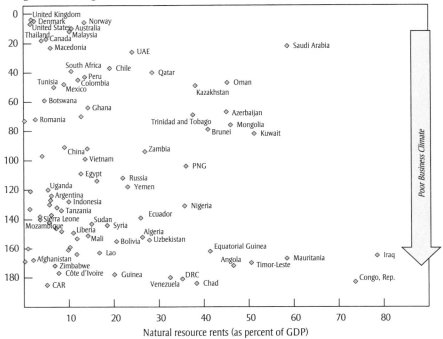

Sources: See figure 7-2.

transfers. Whereas many governments face popular protests (even riots) when they attempt to reduce subsidies, the Iranian authorities managed the transition by creating bank accounts for all citizens and transferring funds intended to compensate for the price hikes. Cleverly, they kept the funds frozen until the subsidies were removed, thus creating public clamor *for* removing subsidies—essentially turning the political dynamics on their head.[12] India recently announced similar plans to swap out a range of public subsidies with cash payments.[13] A recent study estimates that doing a "dividend-subsidy swap" leading to the gradual elimination of most energy subsidies in Egypt in favor of transfers could cut

12. Guillaume, Zytek, and Farzin (2011).

13. Gupta Surojit, "Cash Transfer Subsidy Could Save Rs 60,000 Crore: Study," *The Times of India,* April 1, 2013; "Direct Cash Transfer of Subsidies through Aadhaar from January 1," *The Hindu,* November 24, 2012.

FIGURE 7-6. Business Climate and Resource Abundance

Doing Business ranking (out of 185 countries)

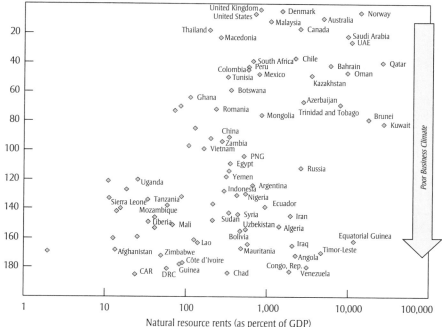

Natural resource rents (as percent of GDP)

Sources: See figure 7-2.

the public deficit by almost 1.5 percent of GDP, and provide a net income boost for the poor.[14]

Is Oil-to-Cash Politically Feasible?

Convincing leaders of oil-rich countries to give up easy money and subject themselves to public scrutiny is difficult in the best of times. There are places, however, where this option is not only fathomable but could even be politically appealing. A number of countries are already implementing resource-backed cash transfers, and others have toyed with the idea. What made it possible in these countries, and what could convince politicians elsewhere to try it?

14. West (forthcoming).

FIGURE 7-7. **Cost of Subsidy of Petroleum Products, Selected Countries, 2011**

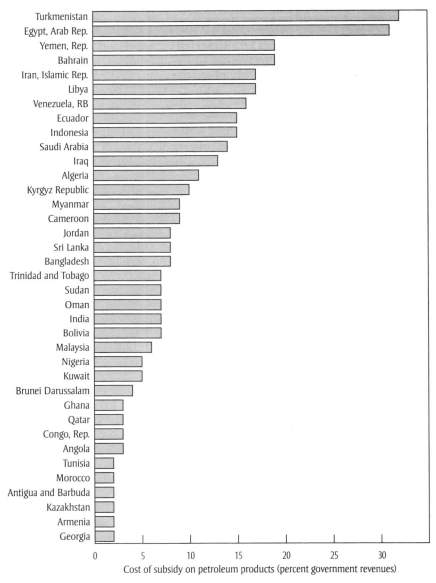

Cost of subsidy on petroleum products (percent government revenues)

Source: IMF (2013).

TABLE 7-2. **Pretax Subsidies as a Percentage of Government Revenues, Selected Countries, 2011**[a]

	Resource				
Country	Petroleum products	Electricity	Natural gas	Coal	Total[b]
Turkmenistan	31.8	12.3	78.5	—	122.6
Uzbekistan	0.1	14.2	46.9	—	61.2
Iran	17.0	14.5	19.5	0.0	50.9
Egypt	30.6	10.4	7.3	0.0	48.3
Zimbabwe	—	47.0	—	—	47.0
Bangladesh	7.6	22.1	13.5	0.0	43.1
Pakistan	1.0	10.2	19.9	0.0	31.1
Bahrain	19.0	9.1	—	—	28.0
Algeria	10.8	2.7	13.5	0.0	27.1
Kyrgyz Republic	10.4	16.3	—	—	26.7
Yemen	19.0	5.4	—	—	24.5
Libya	16.6	4.8	1.5	0.0	23.0
Jordan	8.1	14.4	—	—	22.5
Zambia	0.0	21.6	—	—	21.6
Venezuela	15.8	2.9	1.7	—	20.4
Cameroon	8.9	11.4	—	—	20.3
Lebanon	0.3	19.0	—	—	19.3
Saudi Arabia	14.0	4.7	0.0	0.0	18.7
Indonesia	14.5	3.7	0.0	0.0	18.2
Ghana	3.2	14.7	—	—	17.9
Mozambique	0.0	16.4	—	—	16.4
United Arab Emirates	1.4	5.3	9.6	—	16.3
Ecuador	15.4	0.4	0.0	0.0	15.9
Iraq	12.7	1.8	0.3	0.0	14.8
Oman	7.3	1.8	5.3	—	14.4
Côte d'Ivoire	0.0	13.4	—	—	13.4
Ukraine	0.0	3.8	8.5	—	12.3
Sri Lanka	8.0	3.3	0.0	0.0	11.3
Kuwait	4.6	4.3	1.9	0.0	10.8
Senegal	0.0	10.1	—	—	10.1

Source: Hasnain and others (2013).

a. For a full list of the IMF estimates and for the methodology, see IMF, "Energy Subsidy Reform," 2013.

b. Owing to lack of data, "total" subsidy levels are not strictly comparable across countries. A dash indicates data are not available for a particular country.

A number of characteristics might in theory facilitate the political implementation of a cash transfer scheme.[15] A few are described below.

New rents. Countries that have not yet received oil income may be good candidates for Oil-to-Cash, since vested interests are presumably less entrenched. New discoveries, or potentially a substantial expansion of existing resources, may mean that existing interests who would lose access to rents if dividends were instituted are likely to be less powerful. Grand expectations about personal benefits from new revenues might still exist, but potential gains are unlikely to engender the vigorous defense that vested interests mount. The wave of new oil and gas discoveries across Africa means that a number of countries will soon join the ranks of oil producers. Ghana has only recently started producing oil, while Tanzania, Kenya, and Uganda have yet to kick-start production. Liberia, Sierra Leone, and Somaliland are currently exploring for oil and could find commercially viable reserves, but significant revenues are far in the future. Even in longtime producers like Iraq and Venezuela, a substantial expansion of production could provide a window of opportunity to implement Oil-to-Cash: dividends would be principally financed by incremental income, leaving interests entrenched in existing production untouched. Although using only surplus production makes Oil-to-Cash more politically palatable, it carries one significant risk: it is unlikely to generate incentives to expand taxation, therefore undermining one of the dividend's accountability mechanisms.

This is not to say that once the first drop of oil starts flowing, the opportunity for a dividend system is gone. In fact, countries that have yet to experience the mismanagement of oil revenues will be prone to believe in their own immunity to the resource curse. Therefore, countries that have firsthand experience with wasted oil and mineral revenues may very well be more likely to opt for a system that limits government discretion by tying its hands. Support for the Alaska dividend was due in part to the lightning speed with which the initial oil royalties disappeared without anything to show for them. Countries like Ghana that originally dismiss the idea of Oil-to-Cash may be more receptive if they too prove unable to avoid the resource curse.

New political order. As new governments emerge after a coup, revolution, or conflict, they may seek to change the political order and ben-

---

15. A lot of the following factors come from Gillies (2010).

efit from a (probably brief) window for doing something new. This is arguably the case for Timor-Leste, Iraq, South Sudan, and Liberia. Similarly, mulling over constitutional changes could promote some rethinking of how the state relates to society. The Arab Spring countries, some of which will eventually draft new constitutions, likely fall into this category. Not only do new political orders provide political space for new ideas, writing new constitutions presents an opportunity to enshrine national ownership of natural resources as the principle behind the direct distribution of oil and mineral revenues.[16]

Majority matters. Leaders of resource-rich countries often use rents strategically to consolidate their hold on power, and are therefore more likely to adopt a universal cash transfer scheme when they value—or require—the support of a broad electorate that would benefit from the policy. A competitive democracy (or other broad-based system in which the majority determines political outcomes) is likely more conducive to direct distribution of rents. The two major Mongolian parties both sought to win popular support in the 2007 elections by offering large payments (between $880 and $1,300, almost double the annual per capita income) to all citizens from the country's large untapped mineral deposits.[17] Bolivia's Bonosol program was similarly introduced and approved by President Sánchez de Lozada just months before the 1997 elections as a way to garner support. One hypothesis is that the more democratic a country is, the more likely incumbents should be to favor distribution as a way to consolidate political support (see figure 7-8).

Opposition politics. Perhaps even more likely, opposition leaders—who by definition lack access to oil revenues, and thus have little to lose from a dividend program—could propose Oil-to-Cash to gain the support necessary to beat the incumbent. This happened in Kazakhstan, when the opposition party Ak Zhol proposed distributing 75 percent of all extractive taxes directly to citizens as part of its platform for the 2004 parliamentary elections. Party leader Oraz Jandosov claims that the proposal was well received by the electorate, earning the newly formed party second place in the election.[18] During the 2009 presidential campaign in

16. Gillies (2010, p. 4).
17. John C. K. Daly, "Mongolia's Political Crisis and Its Mineral Riches," *CACI Analyst,* July 23, 2008.
18. Oraz Jandosov, "Kazakhstan Has Already Attempted Redistributing Extractive Revenues," *Financial Times Letters,* June 9, 2009.

FIGURE 7-8.   Voice and Accountability and Resource Abundance

Voice of Accountability Index (2011, percentile rank)

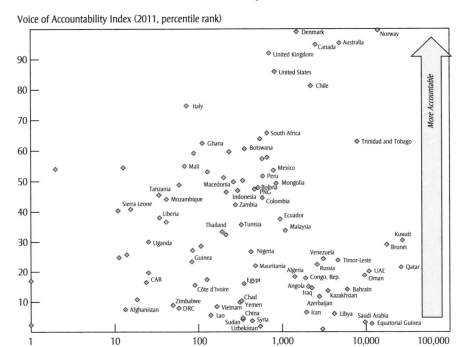

Natural resource rents (USD per capita, log scale)

Sources: See figure 7-2.

Iran, opposition leader Mehdi Karroubi also proposed sharing oil company stock and profits with every Iranian citizen over the age of eighteen as a way to extend public ownership of the country's oil wealth.[19] The opposition in Venezuela has similarly dabbled with distributive ideas.[20]

Postconflict consolidation. Oil-to-Cash can help generate or repair a sense of national belonging following a period of conflict. Cash transfers represent tangible benefits for remaining part of the state and accepting the new political order. They may also help secure a peace deal by ensuring buy-in from a secessionist group. West has argued that such a system in post–Saddam Hussein Iraq could be a way to garner support from the

19. "Iran's Presidential Election: No Certain Outcome," *The Economist,* June 4, 2009.

20. Rodriguez Sosa and Rodriguez Pardo (2012).

Kurds for a unified Iraqi state.[21] In Nigeria, where revenue distribution is a source of regional friction and where social and cultural fissures persist, a universal dividend may also help bind all citizens together and promote national unity. Direct distribution might even provide potentially rebellious or violent groups with a direct stake in peaceful production of natural resources. Other oil-rich, conflict-prone countries, such as Afghanistan, Libya, and Colombia—or Liberia, if it discovers oil—might be tempted to follow suit.[22]

Political legacy. Oil-to-Cash could be politically viable in cases where leaders are seeking to improve their reputation or build a legacy. This could appeal to the vanity of entrenched leaders, such as Equatorial Guinea's Teodoro Obiang, who has already deployed an army of publicists. If Obiang is willing to fund a UN prize in his name to burnish his reputation, then perhaps a dividend in his name is not far behind? More likely—and probably more in line with the ideals of oil to cash—would be a political leader who is seeking to bind a successor and ensure that progress is not lost after a windfall arrives. Certainly former Alaskan governor Jay Hammond viewed the dividend as a way to keep future governors in check. In a contemporary case, Liberian president Ellen Johnson Sirleaf, who is unlikely to be in power by the time significant resource revenues start to flow, may want to create a universal cash transfer to build a lasting and politically unassailable legacy, as well as to minimize the risk that future governments will mismanage oil and mineral revenues.

Summary

Given these economic and political factors, which countries are the most promising Oil-to-Cash candidates? By standardizing and averaging the three economic factors for which data are available—resource abundance, corruption, and business climate—it is possible to generate a tentative list

---

21. West (2011).

22. There is growing support among certain political circles in Iraq for this kind of proposal; see West (2011). In "Generating Skilled Self-Employment in Developing Countries: Experimental Evidence from Uganda" (2013), Blattman, Faila, and Martinez found that one-time cash payments for young adults who wrote a business proposal had a positive economic impact, but had no measurable effect on social cohesion. However, this one-time business-related cash injection seems fundamentally different from the Oil-to-Cash model, which is predicated on a regular dividend.

of the countries that could benefit most from transferring oil or other resource rents to citizens. Table 7-3 shows twenty-five countries that have high resource income per capita, poor business climates, and the highest levels of perceived corruption (see appendix 7A for a full list).[23] By no means inclusive, this list provides a helpful first cut of countries where the economic benefits of Oil-to-Cash would be greatest.

Political factors are much harder to quantify. Existing data (such as measures of democracy) are imperfect indicators of where the Oil-to-Cash idea could take hold. Identifying good candidates requires a deeper understanding of a country's political economy dynamics. Much depends on rapidly changing events, or on identifying potential champions who, like Alaska's Jay Hammond, might embrace the idea and implement it. These political factors, however, can help identify windows of opportunity during which countries could potentially roll out Oil-to-Cash.

Accordingly, we can think of countries along two dimensions: countries that are already economic candidates and those for which there appear to be political windows of opportunity. Countries that meet both conditions, such as Venezuela, are the most promising current candidates; those that lack the political opening, such as Equatorial Guinea (barring a legacy angle), are potential future candidates.

Candidates

Best Economic Case: Venezuela

Venezuela may be a perfect economic candidate for the direct distribution of oil revenues: it has the world's largest reserves of oil per head, a notoriously unaccountable and opaque budget (scoring 37 out of 100 on the 2012 Open Budget Index),[24] high levels of perceived corruption

23. Resource rents per capita is a measure of total natural resource rents produced in a country divided by population from the World Bank's World Development Indicators. This measure is not equivalent to fiscal revenues, although it should give a hypothetical estimate of the potential revenues countries could distribute to each citizen if the government captured all the rents. The average is a simple geometric mean of the three indicators, each of which is standardized following the methodology of the UN's Human Development Index. All three are equally weighted. For a full list, see appendix 7A.

24. Open Budget Index, "Venezuela" (http://internationalbudget.org/wp-content/uploads/OBI2012-VenezuelaCS-English.pdf).

TABLE 7-3. Top 25 Economic Candidates for Oil-to-Cash

Country	Average of standardized economic indicators[a]	Total natural resource rents (USD per capita, 2007–2011 average)[b]	IFC's Doing Business ranking (2012)	WGI Control of Corruption Indicator (P-rank, 2011)
Equatorial Guinea	92.6	11,711.1	162	1.9
Venezuela	89.9	3,083.7	180	7.6
Libya	89.2	4,184.1		4.7
Angola	88.7	2,251.3	172	3.8
Republic of the Congo (Brazzaville)	87.4	1,894.2	183	11.8
Iraq	86.2	2,052.1	165	7.1
Gabon	84.0	4,630.7	170	23.7
Chad	82.8	326.9	184	6.6
Uzbekistan	80.6	543.2	154	4.3
Iran	78.9	1,942.6	145	18.5
Sudan	76.6	338.1	143	5.2
Democratic Republic of the Congo	75.8	58.2	181	3.3
Guinea	75.7	83.3	178	8.5
Côte d'Ivoire	74.8	90.8	177	12.3
Ecuador	74.7	946.1	139	21.3
Russian Federation	74.6	2,598.9	112	13.3
Syria	74.2	436.6	144	17.5
Lao People's Democratic Republic	74.2	140.1	163	13.7
Nigeria	74.2	423.5	131	9.0
Algeria	73.5	1,410.3	152	34.6
Zimbabwe	73.2	49.4	172	5.7
Mauritania	72.7	477.5	167	34.1
Cameroon	72.2	126.3	161	18.0
Yemen	70.8	311.9	118	8.1
Ukraine	70.7	215.1	137	17.1

Sources: Authors' calculations from the World Bank's World Development Indicators, Doing Business rankings, and World Governance Indicators.

a. The average is the geometric average of the three other indicators standardized so that 100 is the worst performer and 0 the best performer on each indicator. Doing Business rankings are unavailable for Libya. Whenever one of the indicators is unavailable (see full list in appendix 7A), the average is the geometric mean of the available indicators.

(it ranked 160 out of 177 countries on Transparency International's 2013 Corruption Perceptions Index),[25] an awful business environment (it ranked 181 out of 189 on the World Bank's Doing Business 2014 indicators),[26] and costly fuel subsidies. Venezuela's economy and government are both highly dependent on oil: oil accounted for 27 percent of GDP in 2012[27] and for more than 60 percent of government revenues from 2004 to 2009.[28] Since poor business environments, oil dependence, and weak administrative capacity undermine the returns to public investment, Venezuela could benefit significantly from transferring some portion of natural resource revenues to citizens.

In fact, Venezuela already does. The Hugo Chávez government distributed a significant portion of the country's oil wealth to the poor through its Misiones Bolivarianas—government social programs. The executive runs the Misiones independently from the ministries and funds them with off-budget oil revenue (only about a third of Venezuela's oil revenue goes through the budget).[29] There are currently thirty-two Misiones, in areas as disparate as music and the arts, agriculture, housing, education, health, job training, and even energy efficiency.

In theory, the Misiones are a mechanism for distributing oil wealth to the poor. In practice, they are notoriously inefficient, ineffective, and more important, extremely politicized—allegedly more a system of clientelism than a social safety net. For instance, Misión Mi Casa Bien Equipada featured the highly publicized distribution of more than a million subsidized Chinese-made refrigerators, washers, and other appliances to Chávez supporters. Even more conspicuously, in the run-up to the 2012 presidential election Chávez announced the creation of two new Misiones—including one named "7 de octubre," the date of the election—intended to mobilize Misión beneficiaries to support Chávez's reelection campaign.

Compared to the discretionary use of oil money by the Chávez government through the Misiones, universal distribution would depoliticize

25. Transparency International, "Venezuela," Corruption Perceptions Index (http://www.transparency.org/country#VEN).
26. International Finance Corporation, "Venezuela," Doing Business (http://www.doingbusiness.org/data/exploreeconomies/venezuela/).
27. World Bank, World Development Indicators (http://data.worldbank.org/datacatalog/world-development-indicators).
28. Rodriguez, Morales, and Monaldi (2011).
29. Rodriguez, Morales, and Monaldi (2011).

oil revenue spending, broaden the tax base, and alter the relationship between the government and its citizens. Instead of receiving charitable handouts from the government in exchange for political support, Venezuelans would receive a dividend from their resource wealth, pay taxes, and hold the government accountable for providing public services in return.

A political opening? Hugo Chávez's death in early 2013 may have provided Venezuela with precisely the kind of regime turnover or constitutional moment that could enable the country to adopt an Oil-to-Cash system. Chávez dominated every aspect of Venezuelan politics for several decades, and his death left a political vacuum that gives the opposition a fighting chance. Although the opposition did not win the rushed election immediately following Chávez's death, his successor, Nicolás Maduro, lacks Chávez's control over the base, which means that the next election could provide a real window of opportunity for the opposition. One thing is clear: the Venezuelan opposition cannot win on the premise of going back to the pre-Chávez era, when economic power was concentrated in the hands of the elite. To have a chance, the opposition will have to appeal to Chávez's base, and provide tangible benefits to all citizens from the country's vast oil wealth. Leaders vying for support could continue the legacy of distributing oil revenues to the people but, in lieu of the discretionary Misiones, do so through transparent, universal, and nondistortionary transfers. One concrete proposal following the Oil-to-Cash model is already circulating among Venezuelan policymakers (see box 7-2). Following the demise of the "Bolivarian revolution," the principle that oil revenues belong to the entire Venezuelan polity, not just those supporting the president, could be enshrined in a new constitution.

Best Political Case: Liberia

A different kind of candidate for the direct distribution of natural resource revenues is very low-income, postconflict Liberia. With a GDP per capita of less than U.S. $400 per year, Liberia is among Africa's poorest countries and is still recovering from a fourteen-year civil war that wiped out most of the existing infrastructure and killed as many as one in ten Liberians. An influx of natural resource revenues could end up wasted, stolen, or diverted to personal projects. In the worst-case scenario, weak management of oil revenues could reignite the Liberian conflict.

B O X   7 - 2 .   El Fondo Patrimonial Venezolano—Venezuelan Patrimonial Fund

Two Venezuelan economists, the father-and-son pair Pedro Luis Rodríguez Sosa and Luis Roberto Rodríguez Pardo, have proposed moving toward a system of oil dividends as a way to cut back the discretionary power of the central government in the use of the oil resources. Because oil revenues flow directly to the government, citizens are passive recipients of government largesse, which has resulted in inefficient patronage spending and has concentrated power in the hands of the ruling party. To give citizens rightful ownership over their resources and reverse the flow of oil revenues from citizens to government, Rodríguez Sosa and Rodríguez Pardo (2012) have proposed the creation, through constitutional mandate, of a savings and stabilization fund under the direct ownership of all Venezuelan citizens. What they call the Venezuelan Patrimonial Fund would have the following characteristics:

—*All revenue from oil would be deposited in the fund.* This includes all income taxes, royalties, windfall taxes, and any other source of revenue associated with the oil industry. In turn, the fund would pay a percentage of the annual oil income (averaged over five years to stabilize against the volatility of oil prices) to the government budget. The percentage could be high initially (80–90 percent) to avoid a fiscal cliff, but would eventually be decreased to 50 percent of the income.

—*Independent and transparent administration.* The fund would be administered by an independent board of directors and be subject to legislative oversight, to monitoring by the comptroller general of the Republic, and to an annual independent audit by an international financial institution or investment bank.

—*Investment.* The capital saved in the fund would be invested in a diversified portfolio of overseas financial assets, with a primary objective to minimize risk and a secondary objective to maximize medium- and long-term return on investment. The purchase of Venezuelan government-issued bonds would be explicitly forbidden.

—*Individual accounts owned by citizens.* Capital and returns accumulated in the fund would be under the personal ownership of every Venezuelan citizen over the age of eighteen through an individual account set up in his or her name. The full balance of the bank account would be available to citizens on reaching retirement age, to complement personal pension savings. Prior to retirement, citizens would be allowed to access a limited amount of capital in their accounts for specific uses, possibly for health care and education expenditures.

—*Transparency.* All Venezuelans over the age of eighteen would have access to information regarding the balance of their accounts from ATMs, over the Internet, and in bank branches. The information would detail total oil revenues received, "taxes" paid to the government, accrued interest, and total account balance.

Despite significant growth since the end of the war, Liberia's economy remains largely made up of subsistence agriculture and natural resource extraction. Timber, iron ore, gold, and rubber account for most exports. Agriculture, fisheries, and forestry made up 72 percent of GDP in 2011, but this figure is projected to decrease as mining takes off, expanding from 1 percent of GDP in 2011 to a projected 20 percent by 2015.[30]

30. *African Economic Outlook* (2013).

The Liberian manufacturing sector accounts for only 7 percent of GDP and is hamstrung by inadequate infrastructure, including few paved roads, few ports, and a crippling lack of electricity. Fewer than 10 percent of people living in the capital and less than 2 percent of Liberia's rural population have access to electricity. At $0.5 per kilowatt-hour, the cost of electricity is three times more than the West African average.[31] While investment in infrastructure is crucial to easing business constraints, there are few guarantees that if the government hits the oil jackpot, it will have the capacity to manage a successful investment strategy.

Liberia does not currently produce oil. But since Ghana's offshore discovery, oil companies, including Chevron, Anadarko, and Tullow, have been signing exploratory agreements, hoping to find oil in Liberia as well. As of the time of writing, several wells had been drilled without success. Chevron's presence and $15 million commitment to Liberia over five years, however, have raised expectations that oil will eventually be found. With expectations already high, the continued stability of Liberia rests on ensuring that the government manages any oil wealth wisely. Liberia was the first African country to comply with the Extractive Industries Transparency Initiative (EITI) guidelines; transparency and governance indicators have greatly improved, albeit from a very low base. This bodes well for Liberian management of natural revenues but is highly dependent on the goodwill of the current government.

Finding a way to manage natural resource revenues well early is all the more important because the structure of oil and mining deals means that it will be years before the government receives significant oil money. Even if Chevron finds oil today, it could take eight to ten years before the company could start exporting in commercial quantities, and even longer before oil companies would be able to write off their capital investment and significant oil revenues would start flowing to the government. Even in mining, where revenues have been steadily increasing as initial capital is repaid, new multi-billion-dollar investments will restart the clock on capital investment write-offs and push significant revenues another five to eight years into the future. This means that the bulk of mineral and potentially oil revenues will flow not to this administration but to the next.

31. USAID (2013).

President Ellen Johnson Sirleaf is a widely admired and respected figure, credited with securing peace under tremendously difficult circumstances and slowly beginning to rebuild the country. Yet Sirleaf knows that her government will not be the one to spend whatever wealth lies under Liberian waters. She may therefore want to find a way to prevent future governments from squandering what money comes in. Establishing a system of cash transfers linked to natural resource revenues and explicitly tied to future oil revenues could not only secure Sirleaf's legacy but keep future governments on a straight path when it comes to spending oil wealth.

Poverty in Liberia is pervasive and extreme: more than four in five Liberians live on less than $1.25 a day, while more than nine in ten live on less than $2 a day. Small cash transfers can therefore make a big difference. A pilot program in Bomi County that made regular payments to labor-constrained poor households confirmed this: schooling among recipients was seven percentage points higher than in families that did not receive any cash, and recipients were twice as likely to report improved health and health care access as nonrecipients. Ninety percent of beneficiaries reported that their families ate more—compared to 26 percent of nonrecipients—with twice as many households eating two or more meals a day as those that did not receive any cash. Ninety-three percent of the cash transfers were reportedly spent locally, which created local markets with multiplier effects for the community.[32]

Liberia's war-torn history also means that a universal dividend could help build unity and discourage renewed violence. The potential to distribute cash to all citizens, however, will depend on future revenues, which are still highly uncertain. If there are no significant oil flows, then some aggregation of other income from mining and timber may be enough to provide a regular stipend. If the amounts are modest, this may require targeting children or the elderly. Demographic targeting maintains the key principle of universality, as citizens would in principle receive transfers at some point in their lives. Universality is crucial, not only because natural resources belong to all citizens and should thus be equally shared but also because targeting by geographic area would be prone to political favoritism and risk reigniting violence. Besides encouraging national cohesion, an oil dividend could also support the creation

32. Miller and Themba (2012).

of a broad tax base, which in turn could provide the basis of a social contract under which taxes are paid in exchange for public services.

Good Candidate: Ghana

Before its oil discovery, Ghana was hailed as a model of economic progress, political openness, and stability in West Africa. In June 2007 a consortium of foreign oil companies announced the discovery of significant oil reserves off the Ghanaian coast (estimates of reserves range from 800 million to 1.8 billion barrels).[33] Oil production began in 2010 in the Jubilee Field, amid warnings of governance and economic threats that would accompany the new influx of oil revenues, possibly stalling or even reversing Ghana's progress.

Oil production has underpinned very high economic growth rates in recent years, but its impact on the welfare of individual Ghanaians remains unclear. Faced with public pressure, Ghana resorted to subsidizing fuel to below cost-recovery levels. IMF-backed attempts to reverse the subsidies have met with strong public resistance.[34] Despite some improvements in revenue collection, Ghana continues to fall significantly behind other low- to middle-income countries, as well as non-oil-producing sub-Saharan African countries, with collected taxes amounting to less than 15 percent of GDP.[35]

Oil production has been disappointing, averaging 67,000 barrels per day in 2011—significantly below the 120,000 target. According to the 2011 EITI reconciliation report, the government received $444 million in revenue from the oil industry in 2011.

In 2011, Ghana passed the Petroleum Revenue Management Act, which establishes a Petroleum Holding Fund at the Bank of Ghana to "receive and disburse petroleum revenue due to the republic," including all royalties, dividends, corporate income taxes, revenue from the national oil company, and any other revenue received directly or indirectly from oil. The law also created the Ghana Stabilization Fund, intended to cushion public expenditures from oil price volatility, and a Heritage Fund, to provide an endowment for future generations when the reserves have been depleted. The share of total oil revenues transferred to

33. See the Natural Resource Governance Institute country information on Ghana (http://www.resourcegovernance.org/countries/africa/ghana/transparency-snapshot).
34. IMF (2012a).
35. IMF (2011).

the government is capped at 70 percent, of which 70 percent must be used for public investment expenditures. The remaining 30 percent of total oil revenues are to be divided between the Stabilization Fund and the Heritage Fund (21 percent and 9 percent, respectively).

The Ghanaian law garnered early praise from watchdog groups for its emphasis on transparency. But gaps between law and practice soon opened, revealing the potential for abuse by politicians. In 2011, neither the budgetary cap nor the set-asides for the Stabilization Fund and Heritage Fund were respected. And while the discrepancies were modest that year, and the government largely adhered to the law, this was not a promising start. Future governments may violate the law more egregiously, threatening stabilization efforts. In 2010, Ghana trailed at the bottom of the Revenue Watch Index—which measures government information disclosure about the oil, gas, and mining industry—together with countries like Equatorial Guinea and Kuwait, which are characterized by "scant revenue transparency." Although Ghana scores above the median on the Natural Resource Governance Institute's 2013 Resource Governance Index,[36] it performs better in theory than in practice: Ghana largely fails to adhere to its own legal framework and disclosure policies (see table 7-4).[37]

Once oil revenue is transferred to the budget, it is subject to the same accountability—or lack thereof—as the rest of the Ghanaian public purse. It is unclear how well the money has been spent, but if other government spending is any indication, there is cause for concern. The World Bank's 2000 Public Expenditure Tracking Surveys found that half of government spending on education (excluding salaries) was unaccounted for, as were 80 percent of nonwage public funds spent on health.[38] A worrying preview of how well oil revenues may be spent is Ghana's experience with Eurobonds. In 2007, Ghana issued a ten-year Eurobond for $750 million, carrying an 8.5 percent interest rate. Where the money ended up is unclear—let alone whether it was invested in a way that justified the hefty interest rate.

36. In 2014 the Revenue Watch Institute merged with the Natural Resource Charter to create the Natural Governance Resource Institute.
37. Revenue Watch (2013); Revenue Watch and Transparency International (2010).
38. Gauthier (2006).

TABLE 7-4. Selected Economic and Governance Indicators for Ghana

Indicator	2008	2009	2010	2011	2012
Macroeconomic indicators					
GDP (current USD billion)	28.5	25.9	32.1	39.5	41.7
GDP per capita (current USD)	1,234	1,097	1,326	1,594	1,646
GDP per capita growth (annual %)	5.7	1.4	5.5	12.4	6.4
Oil rents (% of GDP)			0.3	5.6	5.5
Total natural resources rents					
(% of GDP)	10.6	12.9	13.0	19.0	18.7
Poverty head count (2006)					
U.S. $1.25/day PPP[a]	28.59				
U.S. $2 USD/day PPP	51.84				
National poverty line	28.5				
Revenue and governance indicators					
Revenue Transparency Index (2010)	32.3 (out of 100)[b]				
Resource Governance Index (2013)	63 (out of 100)[b]				
IFC Doing Business ranking (2014)	67 (out of 189)				
IMF Public Investment Management Index	1.87 (median is 1.65)				
WGI Control of Corruption Index (2012)	63 (percentile rank)				
Cost of subsidies (% of gov't revenues, 2011)	17.9				

Sources: For revenue and governance indicators: World Bank (World Development Indicators and World Governance Indicators—Control of Corruption Index, and cost of subsidies); Povcal (source for poverty data), Revenue Watch (Revenue Transparency Index), Natural Resource Governance Institute (Resource Governance Index), International Finance Corporation (Doing Business ranking), and IMF (Public Investment Management Index).
a. PPP denotes purchasing power parity.
b. 100 denotes the most transparent.

Ghana could benefit significantly from an Oil-to-Cash system, which would not only create a broad constituency keen to protect the Stabilization and Heritage Funds but also provide incentives to broaden the tax base, and thus encourage more accountability for overall government expenditures.[39]

While economically desirable, would Oil-to-Cash be politically feasibly in Ghana? The country has been a multiparty democracy since 1992, and has since held five elections widely believed to be free and fair. Ghanaians enjoy freedom of speech and a vibrant civil society, and Ghana is one of few sub-Saharan African countries that can boast improvements in governance indicators. In light of its relative democratic openness, proposing direct dividends may be a politically popular idea

39. Moss and Young (2009).

to pursue and thus feasible either for an incumbent seeking to garner support or for opposition candidates seeking to unseat the ruling party.

Good Candidate: Iraq

A decade after the fall of Saddam Hussein, Iraq is still struggling to consolidate a functional government in the face of strong sectarian tensions. Not least of its many challenges is reaching an agreement on oil. Iraq has yet to pass a hydrocarbon law, let alone devise a coherent spending plan for its oil wealth.[40] Iraq's legacy of bloated bureaucracy, a political system characterized by patronage and rent-seeking, and an economy and regime almost entirely dependent on oil revenues does not bode well for its ability to use oil revenues to diversify its economy and improve social outcomes.[41]

Factors that make Iraq a good candidate for oil dividends are its abundant oil revenues, its poor public investment efficiency, its inexperience with effective accountability, and its significant sectarian tensions.[42] Despite modest improvements since 2003, Iraq falls in the bottom twenty-fifth percentile on all governance indicators. It performs particularly poorly (in the bottom 10 percent) on corruption and rule of law, far below regional and income-group averages.[43] It ranked eighth worst in the world on the International Budget Partnership's Open Budget Index 2012, and an appalling 171 out of 177 countries on Transparency International's 2013 Corruption Perceptions Index.

Although Iraq has exported oil for more than eighty years, a new window of opportunity to introduce a direct distribution of oil revenues could emerge. U.S. policymakers first considered a universal dividend paid to all Iraqis in 2003 and 2004. Because of the political and security climate of the time, the idea was thought too radical. A planned expansion of oil production over the next several years, however, could open the door to a universal oil dividend.[44] A dividend starting at $220 for every Iraqi and rising with expanded production could cut the poverty rate in half (as of 2007, 23 percent of Iraqis lived below the national

---

40. Even though a draft for an Iraqi hydrocarbon law has been under discussion in the Iraqi parliament since 2007, as of June 2013 Iraq had yet to pass it.
41. West (2011).
42. Special Inspector General for Iraqi Reconstruction (2012).
43. Kaufman, Kraay, and Mastruzzi (2010).
44. West (2011).

poverty line), diversify the economy by building local markets, deter secessionist groups, and create a constituency to make government accountable for public expenditures—all without cutting into the government's expenditure plans.[45]

The fact that Iraq is rethinking its constitution as it redefines its oil spending priorities post-Saddam, as well as the existence of a "new revenue" stream from increased production, means that an oil dividend could plausibly be introduced without upsetting entrenched interests. Some powerful political actors in Iraq, including Muqtada al-Sadr and several Shiite parties, may even be amenable to the idea.[46]

Using surplus revenues to distribute a dividend carries a significant risk, however: the government may not feel the need to widen the tax base. If it can continue spending as in the past, the government may prefer to forgo taxes and bypass the accountability taxes bring about, thus potentially undermining a significant benefit of Oil-to-Cash. Yet even without a tax system built around oil dividends, Oil-to-Cash may still carry accountability and efficiency benefits. The abundance of oil revenues suggests that public spending will carry decreasing marginal returns relative to private consumption. This means that Iraq will be better off if citizens, not government agencies, spend the extra money. Furthermore, the portion of oil revenues distributed as dividends would likely come under intense public scrutiny, which could eventually spread to all government expenditures if citizens perceive a trade-off between public spending and their private dividends (as in Alaska). Finally, a well-designed cash transfer system can bring the economic and social welfare benefits reviewed in chapter 2 and help diversify the economy away from oil dependence. All of these factors suggest Iraq would be better off with an oil dividend, even one financed by surplus revenues.

Good Candidate: Mongolia

Mongolia has been among the world's fastest-growing economies in recent years, thanks to the exploitation of its vast mineral deposits. With a population just shy of 3 million, Mongolia's GDP per capita is just

---

45. For projections of what the dividend could look like and an in-depth discussion of its potential benefits, see West (2011). The poverty figures cited are the latest available from the World Bank's World Development Indicators Database (http://data.worldbank.org/data-catalog/world-development-indicators).

46. West (2011).

over $3,000. The economy has been growing at outstanding rates—17 percent in 2011, 12 percent in 2012 and 2013. This mineral-driven growth has translated into concrete benefits for Mongolians, with the poverty rate declining from 39 percent in 2010 to 29 percent in 2011 alone.[47] Imprudent management of natural resource revenues and inefficient public spending, however, are already slowing growth and raising red flags about Mongolia's ability to transform its abundant resource wealth into broad-based and sustained economic development.

Construction of the Oyu Tolgoi copper and gold mine, which sits on one of the largest deposits in the world, began in 2009, while the Talvan Tolgoi coal mine, which holds around 100 years of reserves, is scheduled to begin operations in the next few years. Reserves in these two mines alone are estimated at $1 trillion over the next 50 to 100 years. Mining now accounts for more than 20 percent of Mongolia's GDP and 85 percent of its exports—a resource dependence that will only increase as the mines move into full production.[48] By 2016, mining is expected to contribute more than half of GDP and 95 percent of exports. The impact on fiscal revenues is equally large. In 2011 alone, mineral production contributed $1.7 billion to government coffers, equivalent to almost half of total government revenues.[49]

The magnitude of the flows relative to the Mongolian economy makes it particularly important for Mongolia to protect itself against commodity price volatility. Following advice from Chile, Norway, and international financial institutions, Mongolia set up a number of sovereign wealth funds. One is intended to serve as a stabilization fund and the others to save for future generations or invest in infrastructure. Adhering to fiscal rules designed to stabilize revenues and induce fiscal prudence, however, has proven to be politically untenable. So, despite massive new inflows into the government budget, Mongolia has continued to run fiscal deficits for the past few years. The Fiscal Stability Law that went into effect on January 1, 2013, uses long-run mineral prices to

47. World Bank, World Development Indicators (http://data.worldbank.org/data-catalog/world-development-indicators).

48. Hasnain and others (2013, p. 20).

49. Revenue data are from Mongolia's EITI 2011 report (https://eiti.org/files/Mongolia-2011-EITI-Report-PartI.pdf); total government revenues are from the IMF's 2013 World Economic Outlook database (http://www.imf.org/external/pubs/ft/weo/2013/01/weodata/index.aspx).

estimate revenues and caps the fiscal deficit at 2 percent of GDP. Yet based on spending in the first half of 2013, the fiscal cap is highly unlikely to hold.

While government revenues are projected to triple over the next seven years, attempts to invest the mining bonanza in infrastructure, health, and education have thus far produced mixed results. Mongolia, with its sparse population and subarctic climate, suffers from low connectivity and high unit cost of service delivery, and could use a lot more infrastructure.[50] Since 2005, budget-funded capital expenditures have increased twentyfold, in addition to which Mongolia has recently issued a $1.5 billion sovereign bond to finance road, rail, and energy infrastructure.[51] Unfortunately, results have been disappointing. Corruption is a major concern, underscoring the close ties between and among government, construction, and mining industry circles, as well as murky public contracting and procurement procedures. Poor prioritization and lack of maintenance have led to underinvestment in Ulaanbaatar, Mongolia's capital, while poor capacity to oversee and coordinate projects has resulted in major inefficiencies and poor implementation.[52] Moreover, investments have far outpaced the economy's capacity to absorb them, leading to high inflation, skyrocketing construction costs, and appreciation of the real exchange rate. While the Fiscal Stability Law is supposed to rein in expenditure to avoid overheating of the economy, the government has easily bypassed mandated fiscal caps by financing investment projects off-budget. Without public scrutiny or a powerful constituency, the government has no incentive to comply with the spirit of the law or deliver quality infrastructure investments.

The magnitude of the revenues, combined with inefficient public expenditures, concerns over corruption, and no check on the executive's adherence to stabilization or fiscal rules, makes Mongolia a particularly good candidate for a minerals-to-cash system. In fact, Mongolia is halfway there.

As part of its revenue-spending strategy, Mongolia has been experimenting with national cash transfers that are close in theory, if not in

50. Hasnain and others (2013).

51. Hasnain and others (2013, p. 8).

52. Measured by time and cost overruns alone, the infrastructure investments have produced very low value for the money. The World Bank estimates an average time overrun of 120 percent and a cost overrun of 35 percent (Hasnain and others [2013], p.12).

practice, to the principle of creating citizen shareholders. In 2008 the Mongolian parliament created a Human Development Fund to make every citizen, for the first time in Mongolia's history, equally eligible to own a share of the nation's mineral wealth. The fund was initially expected to provide pension, health, housing, and educational benefits, as well as cash payments. Unfortunately, cash payments were arbitrary in size and frequency and had little connection to the incoming revenue stream. Distributions ballooned to 40 percent of the state budget in 2011, which contributed to inflation. As a result, Mongolia began the process of turning the ad hoc cash payments into regular dividends to all children under the age of eighteen. The future of this program remains highly uncertain.

Reforming Mongolia's cash transfers toward a citizen shareholder principle of oil to cash (with the dividends tied directly to revenues, and then taxed) could provide the political constituency needed to enforce the stabilization fund's fiscal rules, as well as encourage scrutiny over the thus far inefficient public investment. Relatively well-disciplined political parties, with parliamentarians who evidently care about constituents (part of the skewed spending relative to technical priorities can be attributed to the pressure parliamentarians are under to deliver public infrastructure projects to their district),[53] could channel citizen demand for greater government accountability into government oversight.

At a minimum, the Mongolian experience—in which political parties competed to outbid each other on cash transfers and were subsequently under pressure to follow through on their promises—demonstrates the potential popularity of Oil-to-Cash and its political feasibility under a competitive electoral system.

Conclusion

Barring a major disruption in the global economy, a growing number of countries face the prospect of becoming increasingly dependent on natural resource revenues. As a result, managing resource windfalls will remain a pressing issue for governments and citizens across Asia, Africa, and Latin America. Because institutional capacity typically improves at a glacial pace, many countries will struggle to manage their windfall

---

53. Hasnain and others (2013).

gains. This suggests that the pool of potential candidates for Oil-to-Cash will continue to grow. Some variant of universal dividends or a resource revenue–linked national cash transfer program will be implemented somewhere in the near future. It will be an experiment, and many things will go wrong. But other countries will learn from the successes and mistakes of that program, just as we are all now learning from the experiences of Nigeria, Alaska, Mongolia, Ghana, India, and elsewhere. Creating citizen shareholders and putting the wealth of nations into the hands of the true owners, the people, is a powerful idea that deserves attention. Now is the time to put it to the test.

APPENDIX 7A. Oil-to-Cash Candidates along Economic Indicators (All Countries)

Country	Average of standardized economic indicators[a]	Total natural resource rents (USD per capita, 2007–2011 average)[b]	IFC's Doing Business ranking (2012)	WGI Control of Corruption Indicator (P-rank, 2011)
Equatorial Guinea	92.6	11,711.1	162	1.9
Venezuela	89.9	3,083.7	180	7.6
Libya	89.2	4,184.1		4.7
Angola	88.7	2,251.3	172	3.8
Republic of the Congo (Brazzaville)	87.4	1,894.2	183	11.8
Iraq	86.2	2,052.1	165	7.1
Gabon	84.0	4,630.7	170	23.7
Chad	82.8	326.9	184	6.6
Uzbekistan	80.6	543.2	154	4.3
Iran	78.9	1,942.6	145	18.5
Sudan	76.6	338.1	143	5.2
Democratic Republic of the Congo	75.8	58.2	181	3.3
Guinea	75.7	83.3	178	8.5
Côte d'Ivoire	74.8	90.8	177	12.3
Ecuador	74.7	946.1	139	21.3
Russian Federation	74.6	2,598.9	112	13.3
Syrian Arab Republic	74.2	436.6	144	17.5
Lao PDR	74.2	140.1	163	13.7
Nigeria	74.2	423.5	131	9.0
Algeria	73.5	1,410.3	152	34.6
Zimbabwe	73.2	49.4	172	5.7
Mauritania	72.7	477.5	167	34.1
Cameroon	72.2	126.3	161	18.0
Yemen	70.8	311.9	118	8.1
Ukraine	70.7	215.1	137	17.1
Bolivia	69.0	465.5	155	38.9
Guinea-Bissau	68.9	27.4	179	14.2
Suriname	68.8	575.2	164	44.5
Papua New Guinea	68.6	514.9	104	11.4
Central African Republic	67.3	23.8	185	20.4
Indonesia	66.8	294.8	128	28.4
Afghanistan	66.8	13.4	168	1.4
Burundi	66.7	25.3	159	10.9
Togo	65.2	27.5	156	16.6
Philippines	64.3	59.0	138	22.7

(continued)

APPENDIX 7A. **Oil-to-Cash Candidates along Economic Indicators (All Countries)** *(Continued)*

Country	Average of standardized economic indicators[a]	Total natural resource rents (USD per capita, 2007–2011 average)[b]	IFC's Doing Business ranking (2012)	WGI Control of Corruption Indicator (P-rank, 2011)
Egypt	64.2	349.2	109	27.0
Mali	64.2	68.4	151	31.8
Argentina	63.9	661.2	124	42.2
Azerbaijan	63.7	2,768.7	67	10.0
Guyana	63.2	337.7	114	33.2
Senegal	62.4	27.0	166	31.3
Bangladesh	61.6	29.1	129	16.1
India	61.3	88.0	132	35.1
Honduras	61.0	40.9	125	21.8
Benin	60.8	12.8	175	27.5
Pakistan	60.5	55.0	107	15.6
Dominican Republic	60.4	53.7	116	22.3
Tajikistan	60.0	10.9	141	9.5
Haiti	59.7	4.7	174	6.2
China	59.4	337.9	91	30.3
Niger	59.0	9.7	176	28.9
Mongolia	58.9	848.9	76	28.0
Liberia	58.7	34.4	149	39.3
Uganda	58.6	25.4	120	19.9
Bosnia and Herzegovina	58.5	163.4	126	46.4
Burkina Faso	58.4	41.3	153	44.1
Cambodia	58.3	11.3	133	12.8
Mozambique	58.3	41.3	146	41.7
Nicaragua	58.2	30.9	119	24.2
Vietnam	58.0	165.7	99	33.6
Sierra Leone	57.7	15.6	140	26.5
Tanzania	57.6	33.9	134	36.0
Zambia	57.5	276.5	94	37.0
Comoros	57.2	8.7	158	25.6
Ethiopia	56.7	18.5	127	26.1
Kazakhstan	56.6	3,494.6	49	15.2
Paraguay	56.3	40.8	103	25.1
Kuwait	56.0	27,229.2	82	60.2
Brazil	55.4	541.5	130	63.0
Solomon Islands	55.2	200.6	92	40.3
Kyrgyz Republic	55.0	84.9	70	10.4
Trinidad and Tobago	54.9	7,891.3	69	49.8

(continued)

APPENDIX 7A. Oil-to-Cash Candidates along Economic Indicators (All Countries) *(Continued)*

Country	Average of standardized economic indicators[a]	Total natural resource rents (USD per capita, 2007–2011 average)[b]	IFC's Doing Business ranking (2012)	WGI Control of Corruption Indicator (P-rank, 2011)
Kenya	54.9	11.0	121	19.4
Nepal	54.8	20.4	108	23.2
Albania	54.8	128.8	85	32.2
Kosovo	54.7	59.1	98	32.7
São Tomé and Principe	54.4	12.6	160	43.1
Gambia	54.0	11.3	147	37.4
Malawi	53.8	14.1	157	45.5
Swaziland	53.4	58.4	123	50.2
Guatemala	53.2	68.2	93	36.5
Jamaica	51.6	85.0	90	42.7
Morocco	51.0	107.4	97	50.7
Madagascar	50.7	13.9	142	49.3
Timor-Leste	50.4	2.0	169	14.7
Belarus	49.7	121.2	58	24.6
Eritrea	49.6	2.7	182	35.5
Jordan	49.5	123.1	106	59.7
Bhutan	49.3	212.9	148	73.9
Serbia	48.8	177.2	86	55.0
Djibouti	48.0	4.1	171	47.4
Croatia	47.4	208.1	84	58.8
El Salvador	46.8	16.7	113	52.1
Romania	46.8	233.1	72	54.5
Greece	46.2	137.3	78	55.9
Mexico	45.9	789.3	48	45.0
Fiji	45.7	71.7	60	37.9
Brunei Darussalam	45.3	17,679.7	79	77.3
Bulgaria	44.7	1,97.4	66	55.5
Oman	44.7	96,32.2	47	60.7
Belize	44.5	11.6	105	51.2
Sri Lanka	44.2	14.0	81	40.8
Lesotho	44.2	13.4	136	64.5
Colombia	43.3	578.9	45	48.8
Italy	43.1	72.1	73	57.3
Namibia	43.1	68.0	87	64.0
Tunisia	42.4	324.4	50	53.1
Panama	42.1	37.6	61	46.0
Turkey	41.2	66.4	71	61.1

(continued)

APPENDIX 7A. **Oil-to-Cash Candidates along Economic Indicators (All Countries)** *(Continued)*

Country	Average of standardized economic indicators[a]	Total natural resource rents (USD per capita, 2007–2011 average)[b]	IFC's Doing Business ranking (2012)	WGI Control of Corruption Indicator (P-rank, 2011)
Peru	41.1	586.4	43	54.0
Bahrain	40.8	5,966.1	42	64.9
Ghana	40.5	111.7	64	62.6
Czech Republic	40.2	185.8	65	66.8
Costa Rica	40.1	25.9	110	72.0
Moldova	40.1	3.3	83	30.8
South Africa	38.4	659.8	39	59.2
Armenia	37.8	54.7	32	29.9
Saudi Arabia	37.7	9,743.5	22	48.3
Poland	36.9	285.1	55	71.6
Hungary	36.5	110.1	54	67.3
Vanuatu	36.3	15.4	80	67.8
Qatar	34.5	26,175.0	40	80.6
Slovak Republic	33.9	66.4	46	66.4
Botswana	33.9	355.2	59	80.1
Cape Verde	33.6	4.0	122	74.4
Samoa	32.6	8.9	57	61.6
Montenegro	32.2	5.9	51	52.6
Uruguay	32.2	101.3	89	86.3
Macedonia	31.3	262.1	23	56.9
Rwanda	30.9	16.9	52	69.7
Thailand	30.9	192.5	18	43.6
Israel	30.7	133.4	38	73.0
Lithuania	30.0	182.1	27	65.9
Tonga	29.9	1.8	62	47.9
Latvia	29.6	155.6	25	63.5
United Arab Emirates	28.0	10,851.4	26	82.5
Slovenia	26.5	75.9	35	79.1
Malaysia	26.3	1,088.7	12	57.8
Spain	25.9	27.1	44	81.0
Dominica	25.4	2.1	68	73.5
Estonia	24.4	376.1	21	78.7
Portugal	23.4	70.3	30	82.9
Chile	23.1	2,198.5	37	91.9
Bahamas	21.3	3.5	77	89.1
Austria	20.7	179.5	29	89.6
Georgia	19.3	23.2	9	56.4

(continued)

APPENDIX 7A. Oil-to-Cash Candidates along Economic Indicators (All Countries) *(Continued)*

Country	Average of standardized economic indicators[a]	Total natural resource rents (USD per capita, 2007–2011 average)[b]	IFC's Doing Business ranking (2012)	WGI Control of Corruption Indicator (P-rank, 2011)
France	19.1	32.1	34	90.5
Cyprus	18.7	2.0	36	79.6
Belgium	16.5	14.6	33	92.4
Japan	16.4	16.9	24	90.0
Germany	15.6	115.8	20	92.9
Korea, Republic of	15.5	13.0	8	70.1
Ireland	15.2	108.4	15	91.0
Canada	14.8	2,512.0	17	95.3
Luxembourg	14.3	107.7	56	98.1
The Netherlands	13.9	788.0	31	97.6
Switzerland	13.2	19.5	28	95.7
United Kingdom	12.4	703.2	7	91.5
Mauritius	12.3	0.7	19	72.5
United States	11.8	814.8	4	85.3
Australia	11.1	4847.4	10	96.7
Norway	9.0	13,984.5	6	97.2
Finland	7.9	399.1	11	98.6
Sweden	7.4	555.9	13	99.1
New Zealand	3.3	968.1	3	99.5
Denmark	0.0	1,498.8	5	100.0

a. The average measurement is a geometric mean of the three standardized indicators: natural resource rents, doing business, and control of corruption. Each indicator is standardized from 0 to 100 following the methodology of the Human Development Index. The average is standardized so that 100 represents the worst possible score on all indicators and 0 the best.

b. Natural resource rents per capita is a measure of the country's natural resource wealth. It is calculated by the World Bank as the sum of oil rents, natural gas rents, coal rents, mineral rents, and forest rents. Each of those represents the value of the production of these natural resources minus the total cost of production. Of note, this is not equivalent to fiscal revenues from hydrocarbons to the government, which will be lower, as governments capture only a fraction of the total rents.

References

Ablo, Emmanuel, and Ritva Reinikka. 1998. "Do Budgets Really Matter? Evidence from Public Spending on Education and Health in Uganda." Working Paper 1926. Washington: World Bank.

Acemoglu, Daron, Simon Johnson, and James Robinson. 2002. "An African Success Story: Botswana." CEPR Discussion Paper 3219. London: Centre for Economic Policy Research.

Acemoglu, Daron, James Robinson, and Thierry Verdier. 2003. "Kleptocracy and Divide-and-Rule: A Model of Personal Rule." NBER Working Paper 10136. Cambridge, MA: National Bureau of Economic Research.

Agüero Jorge, Michael Carter, and Ingrid Woolard. 2007. "The Impact of Unconditional Cash Transfers on Nutrition: The South African Child Support Grant." Working Paper 39. Brasília: International Poverty Center.

Akee, Randall, William Copeland, Gordon Keeler, Adrian Angold, and E. J. Costello. 2008. "Parents' Incomes and Children's Outcomes: A Quasi-Experiment." IZA Discussion Paper 3520. Bonn: Institut für Zukunft der Arbeit (Institute for the Study of Labor).

Alexeev, Michael, and Robert Conrad. 2009. "The Elusive Curse of Oil." *Review of Economics and Statistics* 91, no. 3: 586-598.

Altunbas, Yener, and John Thornton. 2011. "Does Paying Taxes Improve the Quality of Governance? Cross-Country Evidence." *Poverty and Public Policy* 3, no. 3.

Andersen, Jørgen Juel, and Michael L. Ross. 2013. "The Big Oil Change: A Closer Look at the Haber-Menaldo Analysis." *Comparative Political Studies,* June.

Arezki, Rabah, and Markus Brückner. 2011. "Oil Rents, Corruption, and State Stability: Evidence from Panel Data Regressions." *European Economic Review* 55, no. 7: 955–63.

Arezki, Rabah, Arnaud Dupuy, and Alan Gelb. 2012. "Spend or Send." *Finance and Development* 49, no. 4.

Attanasio, Orazio, Erich Battistin, Emla Fitzsimmons, Alice Mesnard, and Marcos Vera-Hernández. 2005. "How Effective Are Conditional Cash Transfers? Evidence from Colombia." Briefing Note 54. London: Institute for Fiscal Studies.

Attanasio, Orazio, Luca Pellerano, and Sandra Polania. 2008. "Building Trust? Conditional Cash Transfers and Social Capital." London: Institute for Fiscal Studies.

Auty, Richard M. 1993. *Sustaining Development in Mineral Economies: The Resource Curse Thesis*. London: Routledge.

Baird, Sarah, Craig McIntosh, and Berk Özler. 2009. "Designing Cost-Effective Cash Transfer Programs to Boost Schooling among Young Women in Sub-Saharan Africa." World Bank Policy Research Paper 5090. Washington: World Bank.

———. 2010. "Cash or Condition? Evidence from a Cash Transfer Experiment." World Bank Policy Research Paper 5259. Washington: World Bank.

———. 2011. "Cash or Condition? Evidence from a Cash Transfer Experiment." *Quarterly Journal of Economics* 126, no. 4: 1709-1753.

Banerjee, Abhijit V., and Sendil Mullainathan. 2010. "The Shape of Temptation: Implications for the Economic Lives of the Poor." NBER Working Paper 15973. Cambridge, MA: National Bureau of Economic Research.

Barrientos, Armando, and David Hulme. 2008. "Social Protection for the Poor and Poorest in Developing Countries: Reflections on a Quiet Revolution." Brooks World Poverty Institute, University of Manchester.

Barrientos, Armando, and James Scott. 2008. "Social Transfers and Growth: A Review." Working Paper 52. Brooks World Poverty Institute, University of Manchester.

Bell, Joseph, Patrick Heller, and Antoine Heuty. 2010. "Comments on Ghana's Petroleum Revenue Management Bill." Revenue Watch Institute, New York.

Berger, Daniel. 2009. "Taxes, Institutions and Local Governance: Evidence from a Natural Experiment in Colonial Nigeria." Presented at the annual meeting of the Midwest Political Science Association, 67th Annual National Conference. Chicago.

Bird, R., J. Martinez-Vasquez, and B. Torgler. 2008. "Tax Effort in Developing Countries and High Income Countries: The Impact of Corruption, Voice and Accountability." *Economic Analysis and Policy* 38, no. 1: 55–71.

Blattman, Christopher, Nathan Fiala, and Sebastian Martinez. 2013. "Credit Constraints, Occupational Choice and the Process of Development: Long Run Evidence from Cash Transfers in Uganda." World Bank database, enGender Impact. Washington: World Bank.

Bornhorst, Fabian, Sanjeev Gupta, and John Thornton. 2009. "Natural Resource Endowments and the Domestic Revenue Effort." *European Journal of Political Economy* 25:439–46.

Bräutigam, Deborah, Odd-Helge Fjeldstat, and Mick Moore, eds. 2008. *Taxation and State Building in Developing Countries.* Cambridge University Press.

Brunnschweiler, Christa, and Erwin Bulte. 2006. "The Resource Curse Revisited and Revised: A Tale of Paradox and Red Herrings." Working Paper 06/61. Zurich: Swiss Federal Institute of Technology Zurich, Center of Economic Research.

———. 2008. "Natural Resources and Violent Conflict: Resource Abundance, Dependence and the Onset of Civil War." Working Paper 08/78. Zurich: Swiss Federal Institute of Technology Zurich, Center of Economic Research.

Campi, Alicia. 2012. "Mongolia's Quest to Balance Human Development in Its Booming Mineral-Based Economy." Brookings Northeast Asia Commentary 56. Brookings Institution.

Case, Anne. 2001. "Does Money Protect Health Status? Evidence from South African Pensions." NBER Working Paper (8495). Cambridge, MA: National Bureau of Economic Research.

Castro, Patricio, Raúl Junquera-Varela, Osvaldo Schenone, and Antonio Teixeira. 2009. "Evaluation of Reforms in Tax Policy and Administration in Mozambique and Related TA—1994–2007." New York: IMF.

Cavalcanti Tiago, V. de V., Kamiar Mohaddes, and Mehdi Raissi. 2012. "Commodity Price Volatility and the Sources of Growth." International Monetary Fund Working Paper WP/12/12. New York: IMF.

Chandy, Laurence, Kemal Dervis, and Steven Rocker. 2012. "Clicks into Bricks, Technology into Transformation and the Fight against Poverty." Brookings Blum Roundtable. Brookings Institution.

Chronic Poverty Research Centre. 2008. "The Chronic Poverty Report 2008–09: Escaping Poverty Traps." London.

Collier, Paul, and Anke Hoeffler. 1998. "On Economic Causes of Civil War." Oxford Economic Papers 50, pp. 563–73. Oxford University.

———. 2002. "Greed and Grievance in Civil War." Working Paper 2002-01. Oxford University, Centre for the Study of African Economies.

Collier, Paul, Anke Hoeffler, and Dominic Rohner. 2006. "Beyond Greed and Grievance: Feasibility and Civil War." Working Paper 2006-10. Oxford University, Centre for the Study of African Economies.

Costa, Antonio Maria. 2007. "Anti-Corruption Climate Change: It Started in Nigeria." Speech delivered to the 6th National Seminar on Economic Crime in Abuja. United Nations Office on Drugs and Crime.

Croome, David, Andrew Nyanguru, and M. Molisana. 2007. "The Impact of the Old Age Pension on Hunger Vulnerability: A Case Study from the

Mountain Zone of Lesotho." Institute of Southern African Studies, National University of Lesotho.

Dabla-Norris, Era, Jim Brumby, Annette Kyobe, Zac Mills, and Chris Papageorgiou. 2011. "Investing in Public Investment: An Index of Public Investment Efficiency." IMF Working Paper 11/37. New York: IMF.

Davies, Simon, and James Davey. 2007. "A Regional Multiplier Approach to Estimating the Impact of Cash Transfers on the Market: The Case of Cash Transfers in Rural Malawi." *Development Policy Review* 26, no. 1: 91–111.

de Carvalho Filho, Irineu. 2008. "Household Income as a Determinant of Child Labor and School Enrollment in Brazil: Evidence from a Social Security Reform." IMF Working Paper. New York: IMF.

De Janvry, Alain, Federico Finan, and Elisabeth Sadoulet. 2009. "Local Electoral Incentives and Decentralized Program Performance." University of California, Berkeley.

De La O, Ana. 2011. "Do Conditional Cash Transfers Affect Electoral Behavior? Evidence from a Randomized Experiment in Mexico." *American Journal of Political Science* 57, no. 1: 1–14.

Department for International Development (DFID-UK). 2011. "Cash Transfer Literature Review." London. April.

Devarajan, Shantayanan, Helene Ehrhart, Tuan Minh Le, and Gael Raballand. 2011. "Direct Redistribution, Taxation, and Accountability in Oil-Rich Economies: A Proposal." Working Paper 281. Washington: Center for Global Development.

Devarajan, Shantayanan, and Marcelo Giugale. 2013."The Case for Direct Transfers of Resource Revenues in Africa." Working Paper 333. Washington: Center for Global Development.

De Walque, Damien, William H. Dow, Rose Nathan, Carol Medlin, and RESPECT Study Team. 2010. "The RESPECT Study: Evaluating Conditional Cash Transfers for HIV/STI Prevention in Tanzania." Washington: World Bank.

Dixon, Adam, and Ashby Monk. 2011. "What Role for Sovereign Wealth Funds in Africa's Development?" Oil-to-Cash Initiative Background Paper. Washington: Center for Global Development.

Duflo, Esther. 2003. "Grandmothers and Granddaughters: Old Age Pensions and Intra-Household Allocation in South Africa." *World Bank Economic Review* 17, no. 1: 1–25.

Dupas, Pascaline, and Jonathan Robinson. 2009. "Savings Constraints and Microenterprise Development: Evidence from a Field Experiment in Kenya." NBER Working Paper 14693. Cambridge, MA: National Bureau of Economic Research.

Edmonds, Eric V. 2006. "Child Labor and Schooling Responses to Anticipated Income in South Africa." *Journal of Development Economics* 81:386–414.

Eifert, Benn, Alan Gelb, and Nils Borje Tallroth. 2002. "The Political Economy of Fiscal Policy and Economic Management in Oil Exporting Countries." *Finance and Development* 40, no. 1.

Eubank, Nicholas. 2012. "Taxation, Political Accountability and Foreign Aid: Lessons from Somaliland." *Journal of Development Studies* 48, no. 4: 465–80.

Everest-Phillips, Max. 2010. "State-Building Taxation for Developing Countries: Principles for Reform." *Development Policy Review* 28, no. 1: 75–96.

Fearon, James, and David Laitin. 2003. "Ethnicity, Insurgency and Civil War." *American Political Science Review* 97:75–90.

Filmer, Dean, and Norbert Schady. 2006. "Getting Girls into Schools: Evidence from a Scholarship Program in Cambodia." Washington: World Bank.

Fiszbein, Ariel, and Norbert Schady. 2009. "Conditional Cash Transfers, Reducing Present and Future Poverty." Washington: World Bank.

Foster, Vivien, and Cecilia Briceno-Garmendia, eds. 2010. "Africa Infrastructure: A Time for Transformation." Washington: World Bank, Africa Infrastructure Country Diagnostic.

Frankel, Jeffrey. 2010. "The Natural Resource Curse: A Survey." NBER Working Paper 15836. Cambridge, MA: National Bureau of Economic Research.

Garcia, Marito, and Charity M. T. Moore. 2012. "The Cash Dividend: The Rise of Cash Transfer Programs in Sub-Saharan Africa." Washington: World Bank Group.

Gauthier, Bernard. 2006. "PETS-QSDS in Sub-Saharan Africa: A Stocktaking Study." HEC Montreal and World Bank, AFTKL. Washington.

Gavin, Michael, and Ricardo Hausmann. 1998. "Nature, Development and Distribution in Latin America: Evidence on the Role of Geography, Climate and Natural Resources." Working Paper 378. Washington: Inter-American Development Bank.

Gelb, Alan. 1988. *Oil Windfalls: Blessing or Curse?* Oxford University Press, published for the World Bank.

———. 2010. "Economic Diversification in Resource Rich Countries." Article based on lecture at IMF high-level seminar, "Natural Resources, Finance, and Development: Confronting Old and New Challenges," Algiers, November 4–5 (www.imf.org/external/np/seminars/eng/2010/afrfin/pdf/gelb2.pdf).

Gelb, Alan, and Julia Clark. 2013. "Identification for Development: The Biometrics Revolution." Working Paper 315. Washington: Center for Global Development.

Gelb, Alan, and Caroline Decker. 2011. "Cash at Your Fingertips: Biometric Technology for Transfers in Developing and Resource-Rich Countries." Working Paper 253. Washington: Center for Global Development.

Gelb, Alan, and Sina Grasmann. 2010. "How Should Oil Exporters Spend Their Rents?" Working Paper 221. Washington: Center for Global Development.

Gelb, Alan, Kai Kaiser, and Lorena Viñuela. 2012. "How Much Does Natural Resource Extraction Really Diminish National Wealth? The Implications of Discovery." Working Paper 290. Washington: Center for Global Development.

Gelb, Alan, Silvana Tordo, and Havard Halland. 2014. "Sovereign Wealth Funds and Domestic Investment in Resource Rich Countries: Love Me, or Love Me Not?" World Bank's Economic Premise 133. Washington: World Bank.

Gertler, Paul, Sebastian Martinez, and Marta Rubio-Codina. 2006. "Investing Cash Transfers to Raise Long Term Living Standards." World Bank Working Paper 3994—Impact Evaluation Series 6. Washington: World Bank.

Gervasoni, Carlos. 2006. "A Rentier Theory of Subnational Authoritarian Enclaves: The Politically Regressive Effects of Progressive Federal Revenue Redistribution." Paper presented at the annual meeting of the American Political Science Association. Philadelphia.

———. 2010. "A Rentier Theory of Subnational Regimes: Fiscal Federalism, Democracy, and Authoritarianism in the Argentine Provinces." *World Politics* 62, no. 2: 302–40.

———. 2011. "Democracia, Autoritarismo e Hibridez en las Provincias Argentinas: La Medición y Causas de los Regímenes Subnacionales." *Journal of Democracy en Español* 3.

Gillies, Alexandra. 2010. "Giving Money Away? The Politics of Direct Distribution in Resource-Rich States." Working Paper 231. Washington: Center for Global Development.

Glassman, Amanda, Denizhan Duran, and Marge Koblinsky. 2013. "Impact of Conditional Cash Transfers on Maternal and Newborn Health." Policy Paper 19. Washington: Center for Global Development.

Goldman, Anthony. 2011. "Poverty and Poor Governance in the Land of Plenty: Assessing an Oil Dividend in Equatorial Guinea." Oil-to-Cash Initiative Background Paper. Washington: Center for Global Development.

Goldsmith, Scott. 2012. "The Alaska Permanent Fund Dividend: A Case Study in Direct Distribution of Resource Rent." In Moss, *The Governor's Solution*.

Grosh, Margaret, Carlo del Ninno, Emil Tesliuc, and Azedine Ouerghi. 2008. "For Protection and Promotion, the Design and Implementation of Effective Safety Nets." Washington: World Bank.

Guillaume, Dominique, Roman Zytek, and Mohammad Reza Farzin. 2011. "Iran—Chronicles of the Subsidy Reform." IMF Working Paper 11/67. New York: IMF.

Gylfason, Thorvaldur. 2001. "Natural Resources and Economic Growth: What Is the Connection?" Working Paper 530. Munich: Ifo Institute, Center for Economic Studies.

Haber, Stephen, and Victor Menaldo. 2011. "Do Natural Resources Fuel Authoritarianism? A Reappraisal of the Resource Curse." *American Political Science Review*, February.

Hailu, Degol, and Sergei Soares. 2009. "What Explains the Decline in Brazil's Inequality?" Brasília: International Policy Centre for Inclusive Growth, One Pager 89.

Hammond, Jay. 2012. "Diapering the Devil: How Alaska Helped Staunch Befouling by Mismanaged Oil Wealth. A Lesson for Other Oil Rich Nations," in Moss, *The Governor's Solution*.

Handa, Sudhanshu, Carolyn Huang, Nicola Hypher, Clarissa Teixeira, Fabio V. Soares, and Benjamin Davis. 2012. "Targeting Effectiveness of Social Cash Transfer Programmes in Three African Countries." *Journal of Development Effectiveness* 4, no. 1.

Handa, Sudhanshu, and Benjamin Davis. 2006. "The Experience of Conditional Cash Transfers in Latin America and the Caribbean." *Development Policy Review* 24, no. 5: 513–36.

Hanlon, Joseph, Armando Barrientos, and David Hulme. 2010. "Just Give Money to the Poor: The Development Revolution from the Global South." Hartford, CT: Kumarian Press.

Hasnain, Zahid, Munkhnasan Narmandakh, Audrey Sacks, and Marek Hanusch. 2013. "Mongolia: Improving Public Investments to Meet the Challenge of Scaling Up Infrastructure." PREM East Asia and Pacific Report 74944. Washington: World Bank.

Heuty, Antoine, and Ruth Carlitz. 2009. "Resource Dependence and Budget Transparency." New York: Revenue Watch Institute.

Higgins, Matthew, and Jeffrey G. Williamson. 1999. "Explaining Inequality the World Round: Cohort Size, Kuznets Curves, and Openness." Federal Reserve Bank of New York Staff Report 79. New York: Federal Reserve Bank of New York.

Hodges, Anthony, Khurelmaa Dashdorj, Kang Yun Jong, Anne-Claire Dufay, Uranchimeg Budragchaa, and Tuya Mungun. 2007. "Child Benefits and Poverty Reduction: Evidence from Mongolia's Child Money Programme." Working Paper, Division of Policy and Planning. New York: UNICEF.

Hoffman, Barak D., and Clark C. Gibson. 2005. "Fiscal Governance and Public Services: Evidence from Tanzania and Zambia." Faculty paper, Department of Political Science, University of California, San Diego.

———. 2006. "Political Accountability and Fiscal Governance: Evidence from Tanzania and Zambia." Faculty paper, Department of Political Science, University of California, San Diego.

Holmes, Rebecca. 2009. "Cash Transfers in Post-Conflict Contexts." Project Briefing 39. London: Overseas Development Institute.

Human Rights Watch. 2011. "Angola: Explain Missing Government Funds." Washington, December 21.

International Budget Partnership. 2010. "The Open Budget Survey 2010." Washington.

International Labour Office (ILO). 2008. "Can Low-Income Countries Afford Basic Social Security?" Social Security Policy Briefings, Paper 3. Geneva.

————. 2010. "Effects of Non-Contributory Social Transfers in Developing Countries: A Compendium." Working Paper. Geneva.

International Monetary Fund (IMF). 2005. "Oil Market Development and Issues." Washington.

————. 2007. "The Role of Fiscal Institutions in Managing the Oil Revenue Boom." Washington.

————. 2011. "Revenue Mobilization in Developing Countries." Washington, Fiscal Affairs Department.

————. 2012a. "Ghana: 2011 Article IV Consultation." IMF Country Report 12/201. Washington.

————. 2012b. "Nigeria: 2011 Article IV Consultation." IMF Country Report 12/194. Washington.

————. 2013. "Case Studies of Energy Subsidy Reform: Lessons and Implications." Washington, January 28.

Juul, Kristine. 2006. "Decentralization, Local Taxation and Citizenship in Senegal." *Development and Change* 37, no. 4: 821–46.

Kabeer, Naila. 2009. "Scoping Study on Social Protection: Evidence on Impacts and Future Research Directions." London: Department for International Development.

Kakwani, Nanak, Fábio Veras Soares, and Hyun H. Son. 2005. "Conditional Cash Transfers in African Countries." Working Paper 9. Geneva: International Poverty Centre, United Nations Development Programme.

Kaldor, Mary, Terry Karl, and Yahia Said. 2007. *Oil Wars*. London: Pluto Press.

Karl, Terry L. 1997. *The Paradox of Plenty: Oil Booms and Petro-States*. University of California Press.

Karlan, Dean, and Jonathan Morduch. 2009. "Access to Finance." In *Handbook for Development Economics*, vol. 5, ed. Dani Rodrik and Mark Rosenzweig, chap. 2. Oxford: North-Holland.

Kaufman, Daniel, Aart Kraay, and Massimo Mastruzzi. 2010. World Governance Indicators. Washington: World Bank.

Kenny, Charles. 2006. "Measuring and Reducing the Impact of Corruption in Infrastructure." World Bank Policy Research Working Paper Series 4099. Washington: World Bank.

————. 2007. "Construction, Corruption, and Developing Countries." World Bank Working Paper 4271. Washington: World Bank.

————. 2011. "A Thousand Points of Light." *Foreign Policy Magazine*, July 11.

Laserna, Roberto. Forthcoming. "Beating Poverty with Cash: Lessons from Bolivia." Revenue Watch Draft Paper. New York: Revenue Watch Institute.

Leite, Carlos, and Jens Weidmann. 1999. "Does Mother Nature Corrupt? Natural Resources, Corruption and Economic Growth." International Monetary Fund Working Paper WP/99/85. New York: Revenue Watch Institute.

Mahon, James E. 2004. "Causes of Tax Reform in Latin America, 1977–95." *Latin American Research Review* 39, no. 1: 3–30.

Maluccio, John, Michelle Adato, Rafael Flores, and Terry Roopnaraine. 2005. "Red de Protección Social—Mi Familia: Breaking the Cycle of Poverty." Washington: International Food Policy Research Institute.

Manacorda Marco, Edward Miguel, and Andrea Vigorito. 2009. "Government Transfers and Political Support." NBER Working Paper 14702. Cambridge, MA: National Bureau of Economic Research.

Mark, Monica. 2012. "Nigeria Fuel Subsidy Scheme Hit by Corruption." *The Guardian*, April 19.

McCord, Anna. 2009. "Cash Transfers and Political Economy in Sub-Saharan Africa." Overseas Development Institute Project Briefing 31. London: ODI.

McGuirk, Eoin. 2010. "The Illusory Leader: Natural Resources, Taxation and Accountability." Institute for International Integration Studies Discussion Paper Series 327. Dublin: Trinity College, IIS.

Medas, Paulo, and Daria Zakharova. 2009. "A Primer on Fiscal Analysis in Oil-Producing Countries." International Monetary Fund Working Paper WP/09/56. Washington: IMF.

Mehlum Halvor, Karl Moene, and Ragnar Torvik. 2006. "Institutions and the Resource Curse." *Economic Journal* 116, no. 508: 1–20.

Miller, Candace, and Zione Themba. 2012. "External Evaluation of the Bomi Social Cash Transfer Program." Manuscript. March. Center for Global Health and Development, Boston.

Moore, Charity. 2009. "Nicaragua's Red de Protección Social: An Exemplary but Short-Lived Conditional Cash Transfer Program." Country Study 17. New York: United Nations Development Programme, International Policy Centre for Inclusive Growth.

Moore, Mick. 2007. "How Does Taxation Affect the Quality of Governance?" Working Paper 280. Brighton, UK: Institute of Development Studies.

———. 2008. "Between Coercion and Contract." In Brautigam, Fjeldstad, andMoore, *Taxation and State-Building in Developing Countries*.

Moss, Todd. 2011. "Oil-to-Cash: Fighting the Resource Curse through Cash Transfers." Working Paper 237. Washington: Center for Global Development.

Moss, Todd, ed. 2012. *The Governor's Solution: How Alaska's Oil Dividend Could Work in Iraq and Other Oil-Rich Countries*. Washington: Center for Global Development.

Moss, Todd, and Lauren Young. 2009. "Saving Ghana from Its Oil: The Case for Direct Distribution." Working Paper 184. Washington: Center for Global Development.

ODI and UNICEF. 2009. "Fiscal Space for Strengthened Social Protection in West and Central Africa." Briefing Paper. London.

OECD. 2008. "Governance, Taxation and Accountability: Issues and Practices." DAC Guidelines and Reference Series. Paris.

———. 2013. "Liberia Country Note." *African Economic Outlook 2013: Structural Transformation and Natural Resources*. Paris: OECD Publishing. 242–43.

Paler, Laura. Forthcoming. "Keeping the Public Purse: An Experiment in Windfalls, Taxes, and the Incentives to Restrain Government." University of Pittsburgh.

Peg, Scott. 2009. "Chronicle of a Death Foretold: The Collapse of the Chad-Cameroon Pipeline Project." *African Affairs* 108, no. 431: 311–20.

Pickens, Mark, David Porteous, and Sarah Rotman. 2009. "Banking the Poor via G2P Payments." CGAP Focus Note 58. Washington: Consultative Group to Assist the Poor.

Pritchett, Lant. 2000. "The Tyranny of Concepts: CUDIE (Cumulated, Depreciated, Investment Effort) Is Not Capital." *Journal of Economic Growth* 5:361–84.

Rawlings, Laura, and Gloria Rubio. 2003. "Evaluating the Impact of Conditional Cash Transfer Programs: Lessons from Latin America." World Bank Policy Research Working Paper 3119. Washington: World Bank.

Revenue Watch Institute. 2013. *Resource Governance Index*. New York.

Revenue Watch Institute and Transparency International. 2010. "Revenue Watch Index: Transparency, Governments and the Oil, Gas, and Mining Industries." New York.

Robinson, James, Ragnar Torvik, and Thierry Verdier. 2006. "Political Foundations of the Resource Curse." *Journal of Development Economics* 79: 447–68.

Rodriguez, Pedro L., Jose R. Morales, and Francisco J. Monaldi. 2012. "Direct Distribution of Oil Revenues in Venezuela: A Viable Alternative?" Working Paper 306. Washington: Center for Global Development.

Rodriguez Sosa, Pedro Luis, and Luis Roberto Rodriguez Pardo. 2012. *El Petróleo Como Instrumento de Progreso: Una Nueva Relación Ciudadano-Estado-Petróleo*. Caracas: Ediciones IESA.

Roodman, David. 2012. "Due Diligence: An Impertinent Inquiry into Microfinance." Washington: Center for Global Development.

Ross, Michael. 2001. "Does Oil Hinder Democracy?" *World Politics* 53: 325–61.

————. 2004a. "Does Taxation Lead to Representation?" *British Journal of Political Science* 34: 229–49.

————. 2004b. "What Do We Know about Natural Resources and Civil War?" *Journal of Peace Research* 41, no. 3: 337–56.

————. 2006. "A Closer Look at Oil, Diamonds, and Civil Wars." *Annual Review of Political Science* 9: 265–300.

————. 2009. "Oil and Democracy Revisited." Faculty paper, Department of Political Science, University of California, Los Angeles.

————. 2012. *The Oil Curse: How Petroleum Wealth Shapes the Development of States*. Princeton University Press.

Sachs, Jeffrey, and Andrew Warner. 1995. "Natural Resource Abundance and Economic Growth." NBER Working Paper 5398. Cambridge, MA: National Bureau of Economic Research.

Sala-i-Martin, Xavier, and Arvind Subramanian. 2003. "Addressing the Natural Resource Curse: An Illustration from Nigeria." Working Paper WP/03/139. New York: International Monetary Fund.

Samson, Michael, Una Lee, Asanda Ndlebe, Kenneth Mac Quene, Ingrid van Niekerk, Viral Gandhi, Tomoko Harigaya, and Celeste Abrahams. 2004. "The Social and Economic Impact of South Africa's Social Security System." EPRI Research Paper 37. Cape Town, SA: Economic Policy and Research Institute.

Samson, Michael, Ingrid van Niekerk, and Kenneth Mac Quene. 2011. "Designing and Implementing Social Transfer Programmes." 2nd ed. Cape Town, SA: Economic Policy and Research Institute.

Sen, Amartya. 1999. *Development as Freedom*. New York: Random House.

Shaxson, Nicholas. 2007. *Poisoned Wells: The Dirty Politics of African Oil*. New York: Palgrave Macmillan.

Sinnott, Emily, John Nash, and Augusto de la Torre. 2010. "Natural Resources in Latin America and the Caribbean: Beyond Booms and Busts?" Washington: World Bank.

Soares, Sergei, Rafael Guerreiro Osório, Fábio Veras Soares, Marcelo Medeiros, and Eduardo Zepeda. 2009. "Conditional Cash Transfers in Brazil, Chile and Mexico: Impacts upon Inequality." *Estudios Económicos*, special issue, pp. 207–24.

Special Inspector General for Iraqi Reconstruction. 2012. "Quarterly Report to the United States Congress." October 30.

Stijns, Jean-Philippe C. 2005. "Natural Resource Abundance and Economic Growth Revisited." *Resources Policy* 30, no. 2: 107–30.

Strategic Foresight Group. 2006. "Cost of Conflict in Sri Lanka." Publication 79052. Mumbai, India.

Sultan, Sonya, and Taman Schrofer. 2008. "Building Support to Have Targeted Social Protection Interventions for the Poorest: The Case of Ghana." Paper presented at the conference, "Social Protection for the Poorest in Africa: Learning from Experience." Kampala, Uganda, September 8–10.

Tabatabai, Hamid. 2010. "The 'Basic Income' Road to Reforming Iran's Subsidy System." Paper prepared for the 13th BIEN Conference, São Paulo, Brazil, June 30–July 2.

Tilly, Charles. 1975. *The Formation of National States in Western Europe.* Princeton University Press.

Timmons, Jeffrey F. 2005. "The Fiscal Contract." *World Politics* 57: 530–67.

Tornell, Aaron, and Philip R. Lane. 1999. "The Voracity Effect." *American Economic Review* 89, no. 1: 22–46.

Toto Same, Achille. 2008. "Mineral-Rich Countries and Dutch Disease: Understanding the Macroeconomic Implications of Windfalls and the Development Prospects. The Case of Equatorial Guinea." World Bank Policy Research Paper 4595. Washington: World Bank.

USAID. 2013. "Liberia Energy Sector Support Project." http://liberia.usaid.gov/ LESSP.

Veras Soares, Fabio, Sergei Soares, Marcelo Medeiros, and Rafael Guerreiro Osório. 2006. "Cash Transfer Programmes in Brazil: Impacts on Inequality and Poverty." Working Paper 21. Brasília: International Poverty Center, UNDP/IPEA.

Vincent, Katharine, and Tracy Cull. 2009. "Impacts of Social Cash Transfers: Case Study Evidence from Across Southern Africa." Córdoba: Instituto de Estudos Socialis e Económicos (IESE).

von Soest, Christian. 2008. "Donor Support to Tax Administration in Africa: Experience in Ghana, Tanzania, Uganda and Zambia." DIE Discussion Paper 2/2008. Bonn: DIE (German Development Institute).

Wallis, Joanne, Alexandra Gillies, and Mericio Akara. Forthcoming. "Fahe Hamutuk: Sharing Oil Wealth through Cash Transfer in Timor-Leste." Working Paper. New York: Natural Resource Governance Institute.

Webb, Steven. 2009. "Managing Mineral Wealth in Middle-Income Countries: Political Economy in Five Examples from Latin America." Washington: World Bank.

West, Johnny. 2011. "Iraq's Last Window: Diffusing the Risks of a Petro-State." CGD Working Paper 266. Washington: Center for Global Development.

———. Forthcoming. "Egypt Case Study." CGD Working Paper. Washington: Center for Global Development.

Wietler, Katharina. 2007. "The Impact of Social Cash Transfers on Informal Safety Nets in Kalomo District, Zambia: A Qualitative Study." Lusaka: Zambia Ministry of Community Development and Social Services and German Technical Cooperation.

Williams, Martin. 2007. "The Social and Economic Impacts of South Africa's Child Support Grant." EPRI Research Paper 40. Cape Town, SA: Economic Policy and Research Institute.

Woodward, John D., Nicholas M. Orlans, and Peter T. Higgins. 2003. *Biometrics: Identity Assurance in the Information Age.* Berkeley, CA: McGraw-Hill Osborne Media.

World Bank. 2004. *Unlocking the Employment Potential in the Middle East and North Africa: Toward a New Social Contract.* Middle East and North Africa (MENA) Development Report. Washington: World Bank

———. 2005. "Egypt—Toward a More Effective Social Policy: Subsidies and Social Safety Net." World Bank Paper 33550-EG. Washington: World Bank.

———. 2010. *Global Monitoring Report 2010: The MDGs after the Crisis.* Washington: World Bank.

———. 2011. "Pakistan—Flood Emergency Cash Transfer Project." Washington: World Bank

———. 2014. "Poverty Overview." Washington: World Bank, October 8.

Yablonski, Jennifer, and Michael O'Donnell. 2009. "Lasting Benefits: The Role of Cash Transfers in Tackling Child Mortality." London: Save the Children UK.

Yanez-Pagans, Monica. 2008. "Culture and Human Capital Investments: Evidence of an Unconditional Cash Transfer Program in Bolivia." IZA Discussion Paper 3678. Bonn: Institut für Zukunft der Arbeit (Institute for the Study of Labor).

Zucco, Cesar. 2008. "The President's 'New' Constituency: Lula and the Pragmatic Vote in Brazil's 2006 Presidential Elections." *Journal of Latin American Studies* 40, no. 1: 29–49.

Index

Abacha, Sani (Nigerian general and politician), 36–37

Afghanistan, 73, 129. *See also* Asia

Africa, 7, 27–28, 32, 50, 71, 73, 126. *See also individual countries*

Africa–sub-Saharan: banks and banking in, 87; cash transfer programs in, 9, 20, 21–22, 24, 28; democracy in, 36; poverty rate in, 8; public expenditures in, 92. *See also individual countries*

Ajaokuta steel complex (Nigeria), 48

Alaska, 67, 81, 82, 99, 112. *See also* Hammond, Jay; United States

Alaska Permanent Fund Corporation, 58, 60–62, 67, 99, 112, 126

Algeria, 45, 48, 49, 50. *See also* Africa

Al-Sadr, Muqtada (politician; Iraq), 141

Anadarko oil company, 135

Anderson, Jørgen Juel, 36

Angola, 34, 38, 51, 54, 92. *See also* Africa

Arab Spring (2010), 95, 127

Argentina, 17, 47, 112. *See also* Latin America

Asia, 7, 27, 71, 87. See also *individual countries*

Asia–East, 8, 46. See also *individual countries*

Australia, 2

Autocracies, 35–36

Azerbaijan, 48, 49, 50. *See also* Europe

Bangladesh, 12, 15, 22, 24. *See also* Asia

Bank of Ghana, 137

Banks and banking, 73–74, 87, 109. *See also* Electronic transfers

Bantuan Langsung Tunai (Indonesia), 26

Benin, 46. *See also* Africa

Biometric identification, 71–73, 84–88, 108. *See also* National identification systems

Bolivia, 2; biometric identification in, 87; cash transfer programs in, 15, 27, 60, 65, 66, 67, 68, 100,

Panama, 4, 56. *See also* Latin
America
PANES. *See* Plan de Atención
Nacional a la Emergencia Social
Papua New Guinea, 2, 53, 97. *See
also* Asia
Paraguay, 14–15, 80, 104. *See also*
Latin America
Paris Club, 59
Pemex (oil company; Mexico), 49
Petroleum Fund (Timor-Leste), 59
Petroleum Holding Fund (Ghana), 137
Petroleum Revenue Management Act
(Ghana; 2011), 137
Plan de Atención Nacional a la
Emergencia Social (PANES;
Uruguay), 18
Political issues: cash transfer
programs, 18, 21, 27, 28–31, 60,
61, 80, 82–85, 96, 99; dividends
and distribution, 127; national
unity, 82, 83–84; natural resource
wealth, 32, 36, 96; new political
orders, 126–27; oil prices, 58; oil
revenues, 50, 79; opposition
politics, 127–28; political stability,
17; postconflict consolidation,
128–29; resource curse, 45–51;
stabilization funds, 52, 53, 98;
subsidies, 49–51, 80, 95, 120;
sudden windfalls, 2; taxation, 48,
62; voting, 18. *See also*
Democracy; Elections;
Government; Oil-to-Cash
proposal; Social contract
Poverty: backsliding into, 8; cash
transfer programs and, 10, 20, 22,
24, 79, 81, 95, 101, 103–04;
chronic poverty, 8; definitions of,
7n1, 8; effects of, 10; financial
access and, 87; identification and,
86; inherited poverty, 20; nutrition
and, 12b; paths out of, 14; political
voice and, 17; reductions in, 7–8;

windfalls and, 50. *See also
individual areas and countries*
Prebbisch-Singer hypothesis, 44–45
Pregnancy, 21
Progresa cash transfer program
(Mexico), 10, 17, 18. *See also*
Oportunidades
Productive Safety Nets Program
(Ethiopia), 16
Public Expenditure Tracking Surveys
(World Bank), 138
Public Investment Management
Index (IMF), 115n6, 116, 117
Publish What You Pay network, 54
Pula Fund (Botswana), 99

Red de Protección Social (RPS;
Nicaragua), 29–30
Renta Dignidad (Bolivia), 66, 67
Resource curse: advice to new oil
producers, 51–55; causes of, 51;
dilemma of, 1–2; dynamics of,
40–51; economic mechanisms of,
40–45; forms of, 32n2; mineral
wealth as a, 32; reality of, 33–40;
rent-seeking and corruption and, 3;
solutions for, 2–3, 32. *See also*
Mineral resources; Oil
Resource Governance Index (Natural
Resource Governance Institute),
138
Resource Governance Index
(Revenue Watch Institute), 120b,
121
Revenue Watch Index, 138
Revenue Watch Institute, 120b, 121
Rodriguez Pardo, Luis Roberto, 134b
Rodriguez Sosa, Pedro Luis, 134b
Roodman, David, 87–88
Ross, Michael, 34, 36
RPS. *See* Red de Protección Social
Russia, 97

Sachs, Jeffrey, 33

The Center for Global Development

The Center for Global Development works to reduce global poverty and inequality through rigorous research and active engagement with the policy community to make the world a more prosperous, just, and safe place for us all. The policies and practices of the rich and the powerful—in rich nations, as well as in the emerging powers, international institutions, and global corporations—have significant impacts on the world's poor people. We aim to improve these policies and practices through research and policy engagement to expand opportunities, reduce inequalities, and improve lives everywhere. By pairing research with action, CGD goes beyond contributing to knowledge about development. We conceive of and advocate for practical policy innovations in areas such as trade, aid, health, education, climate change, labor mobility, private investment, access to finance, and global governance to foster shared prosperity in an increasingly interdependent world.

About the Authors

TODD MOSS is the chief operating officer and a senior fellow at the Center for Global Development. His research focuses on U.S.-Africa relations and financial issues facing sub-Saharan Africa. Moss served as deputy assistant secretary at the U.S. Department of State and worked at the World Bank. He is also author of the thrillers *The Golden Hour* (Penguin/Putnam, 2014) and *Minute Zero* (Penguin/Putnam, 2015).

CAROLINE LAMBERT is an award-winning former journalist and visiting fellow at the Center for Global Development. While a staff journalist for *The Economist*, Lambert won several awards for her coverage of Southern Africa's politics and business from Johannesburg. She also reported on conflict and postconflict situations in Algeria, Afghanistan, Liberia, Sierra Leone, and Zimbabwe. Before becoming a journalist, she worked for the World Bank.

STEPHANIE MAJEROWICZ is a PhD candidate in public policy at the Harvard Kennedy School of Government. Her research interests include financial development, labor markets, and resource management. Previously, Majerowicz worked as a research assistant at the Center for Global Development, where she focused on natural resource revenue management, multilateral aid, and fiscal policy in sub-Saharan Africa. She has also worked as a consultant for the World Bank on issues of poverty and inequality in Latin America. She holds a bachelor's degree from Stanford University and a master's degree from Harvard University.

Praise for *Oil to Cash*

Todd Moss, Caroline Lambert, and Stephanie Majerowicz offer a well-argued explanation of how oil-to-cash transfers could help countries overcome the corruption, economic volatility, and lack of government accountability that too often plague countries with rich resources but weak institutions.

—MICHAEL ROSS, author of *The Oil Curse: How Petroleum Wealth Shapes the Development of Nations*

Sharing oil revenues directly with citizens is one of those simple but powerful ideas that could help disrupt the low-level equilibrium that many resource-rich countries find themselves in. This book hits the sweet spot of synthesizing rigorous research on oil-to-cash and engaging readers in a compelling manner.

—SHANTA DEVARAJAN, chief economist for the Middle East and North Africa region, World Bank

An excellent discussion of a game-changing idea that has to be seriously considered by politicians and policymakers in oil exporting countries all around the world.

—FRANCISCO MONALDI, visiting professor of energy policy, Harvard Kennedy School, and director, Center on Energy, IESA, Venezuela

Oil to Cash addresses one of the most puzzling problems in development—how to make sure a country's natural resource wealth is used for the greater good—and advocates for an innovative policy to solve it: direct and transparent distribution of dividends to all citizens.

—ROBERTO LASERNA, CERES researcher and president of Fundación Milenio

Oil to Cash offers thought provoking and practical ideas to restore the social compact between citizens and the governments that manage natural resources on their behalf. It proposes smart policy options to phase out socially regressive and economically wasteful fuel subsidies and replace them with conditional and unconditional transfers to boost human development.

—ANTOINE HEUTY, founder and CEO of ULULA; former deputy director of Revenue Watch Institute

Better and cheaper technologies for biometric identification and financial transfers have made it possible to turn citizens into actual shareholders of their countries' natural wealth—as Alaska has done at the state level. This is especially relevant for Africa, where vast deposits of oil, gas, and minerals were discovered in recent years, and where public institutions have traditionally mismanaged—or worse—the rents coming from extractive industries. Why not give part of those rents directly to the people, especially the poor? That is the question that Oil to Cash dares to ask and brilliantly answers."

—MARCELO GIUGALE, senior director of global practice for macroeconomics and fiscal management, World Bank

Oil to Cash presents a new vision of how citizens in resource-rich countries can take ownership of their oil, gas or mineral wealth and benefit. It should be read by everyone interested in the relationship between resources and development.

—ALAN GELB, senior fellow, Center for Global Development